AF303970

Defoe Abbott Marx Hardy Melville Montaigne Machiavelli Haggard Chesterton Emerson Cooper Austen Hugo Grimm Eliot

Stoker Carroll Christie Molière

Wilde Maupassant Byron Schiller

Garnett Einstein Fitzgerald Engels Smith Kafka Hall

Goethe Hawthorne

Cotton Dostoyevsky Willis

Baum Henry Kipling Doyle

Leslie Dumas Nietzsche

Flaubert Turgenev Balzac

Stockton Vatsyayana Crane

Burroughs Verne

Curtis Tocqueville Gogol Vinci

Homer Widger Tolstoy Whitman Busch

Darwin Thoreau

Potter Freud Twain Scott

Kant Zola Lawrence Plato Harte

Jowett Stevenson Dickens Hesse

Andersen Burton

London Descartes Cervantes

Poe Aristotle Wells Voltaire Cooke

Hale James Hastings

Bunner Shakespeare Irving

Richter Chekhov Chambers

Doré da Shaw Wodehouse Benedict Alcott

Dante Pushkin

Swift Newton

 **tredition®**

tredition was established in 2006 by Sandra Latusseck and Soenke Schulz. Based in Hamburg, Germany, tredition offers publishing solutions to authors and publishing houses, combined with worldwide distribution of printed and digital book content. tredition is uniquely positioned to enable authors and publishing houses to create books on their own terms and without conventional manufacturing risks.

For more information please visit: www.tredition.com

TREDITION CLASSICS

This book is part of the TREDITION CLASSICS series. The creators of this series are united by passion for literature and driven by the intention of making all public domain books available in printed format again - worldwide. Most TREDITION CLASSICS titles have been out of print and off the bookstore shelves for decades. At tredition we believe that a great book never goes out of style and that its value is eternal. Several mostly non-profit literature projects provide content to tredition. To support their good work, tredition donates a portion of the proceeds from each sold copy. As a reader of a TREDITION CLASSICS book, you support our mission to save many of the amazing works of world literature from oblivion. See all available books at www.tredition.com.

Project Gutenberg

The content for this book has been graciously provided by Project Gutenberg. Project Gutenberg is a non-profit organization founded by Michael Hart in 1971 at the University of Illinois. The mission of Project Gutenberg is simple: To encourage the creation and distribution of eBooks. Project Gutenberg is the first and largest collection of public domain eBooks.

Woodward's Country Homes

George E. (George Evertson) Woodward

Imprint

This book is part of TREDITION CLASSICS

Author: George E. (George Evertson) Woodward
Cover design: Buchgut, Berlin – Germany

Publisher: tredition GmbH, Hamburg - Germany
ISBN: 978-3-8472-1707-7

www.tredition.com
www.tredition.de

WOODWARD'S

COUNTRY HOMES,

BY

GEO. E. & F. W. WOODWARD,

ARCHITECTS,

Authors of "Woodward's Graperies and Horticultural Buildings."

— — — — — —

FOURTH THOUSAND.

— — — — — —

NEW-YORK:
GEO. E. & F. W. WOODWARD, 37 PARK ROW,
Office of the HORTICULTURIST.
1866.

STEPHEN HALLET,
PRINTER,
No. 74 Fulton Street.

WOODWARD'S COUNTRY HOMES.

In presenting to the public a new work on Domestic Architecture, it is our aim to furnish practical designs and plans, adapted to the requirements of such as are about to build, or remodel and improve, their Country Homes.

The rapid progress in rural improvement and domestic embellishment all over the land, during the last quarter of a century, is evident to the observation of every traveler, and, as we have found during several years of professional experience, there has grown up a demand for architectural designs of various grades, from the simple farm cottage to the more elaborate and costly villa, which is not supplied by the several excellent works on this subject which are within the reach of the building and reading public.

Among the permanent dwellers in the country this spirit of improvement, fostered as it is by the diffusion of publications in the various departments of Rural Art, and by a wider and more genial general culture as the means of intercommunication and education [8] are increased, is becoming more manifest every year. But besides these intelligent farmers and tradesmen who make the country their home the year round, there is a large class of persons whose tastes or business avocations compel them to reside a considerable portion of the year in our cities or suburbs—prosperous merchants, bankers, professional men, and wealthy citizens—who have the tastes and means to command such enjoyments and luxuries as the country affords; who need the change in scenes, associations, employments and objects of interest, for themselves and their households, and who enjoy, with a keen relish, the seclusion, the comparative freedom from restraint, the pure, sweet air, the broad, open sunshine, and the numerous other rural advantages which are essentially denied them in their city homes.

In former years this class of people resorted, almost exclusively, to the sea-side, and a few popular mineral springs, taking in, perhaps, Niagara in their transit, and rarely venturing into the wild and unexplored regions of Lake George. They returned to town in the early days of September, with many a backward, longing look at

the attractions and delights from which they reluctantly tore themselves away, and settled down again to the weary tread-mill of
business. But for some years past this class has largely increased in
number, and instead of confining themselves to their [9] former
resorts, they now seek the upper country, and prolong their stay
into the glorious days of Autumn. Many of them have provided
permanent summer homes, among the hills and on the lake or river
shores. They have bought, and built, and planted, until they have
identified themselves with the chosen spot, and as their trees have
taken root in the fertile soil, so have their affections taken root in the
beautiful country. They hasten gladly to these rural scenes with the
opening Summer, and they leave them with regret when the exi-
gencies of business require their presence in the city,—when the
Summer suns have ripened the luscious fruits, and the flowers fade
with the frosty kisses of the cold, and the passenger birds fly
Southward. This class of our population know where to find all the
facilities for the best country enjoyments, and their ample means
assure them a free choice of summer resorts, and adequate command of all the appliances of pleasant country living.

But there is another and still larger class of citizens who have neither the means to enable them to keep up both town and country
residences, nor such command of their time that they can pass two
or three months of every summer away from their business. There
are thousands of clerks and subordinate officers in the banking and
insurance institutions in our cities and in our large commercial
houses; there are many merchants [10] who are making their way
slowly and surely to competence and wealth, who would gladly
compromise for one-third of such a summer vacation. These are
men of intelligence, and sometimes of a good deal of social and
intellectual culture and refinement. Many of them were born, and
their boyhood nurtured amongst the hills. They love the country
with the intensity and purity of a first love, and they long for com-
munion once more with nature in all her moods of loveliness. Their
sweetest dreams still, when they forget the hard realities of life, are
of green lawns and sloping hill-sides, of waving trees and cool
streams. And they would wish that their children should become
familiar with the same wholesome associations, and be moved by
the same attachments and inspirations. In the city they are constant-

ly exposed to its excitements, and subjected to the restraints of its artificial modes, with few outward influences to counteract upon their development; with very little, indeed, except the discipline and the affections of home to emancipate them from the tendencies to a trivial, artificial, and sordid life. They would gladly supply to them the healthful tone and vigor—the outer and inner bloom and freshness—which are the product of out-door life in the pure air of the country. But they are compelled by considerations of economy, to forego most of these advantages, and allow their children to [11] grow up with city tastes and habits. They long for the country but think they must content themselves with the town, until the time comes when their fortunes will enable them to command the coveted indulgences.

The time may come, sooner than they anticipate, when they will be obliged to choose the country.

Our towns are rapidly overflowing their local boundaries, and spreading out into suburbs, more or less beautiful and desirable. As far as New York city is concerned, it is simply a question of time how soon our middle-class citizens, who desire to live comfortably, with due regard to economical conditions, will be obliged to choose the country for their homes.

During the last forty years this city has increased in population with a rapid and uniform rate. Within the memory of persons now living, it has grown from an inconsiderable commercial town, until it has become one of the great cities of the world. This rapid stride and steady progress furnish us with the elements for calculating the period when the whole island will be covered with buildings, and there will remain no more vacant space for the use of its commerce, or the domestic accommodation of its citizens. The present population of the city is estimated at fully one million. The entire territorial capacity of the city, the density of the population remaining the same [12] as it is at present, cannot much exceed two millions. The ratio of increase during each period of five years, since 1820, is about twenty-eight per cent. It will thus be seen that the utmost limit of the city's capacity will be reached within the next sixteen or seventeen years, and New York will be a solid and compact city from the Battery to Westchester County.

Meanwhile, the expenses of living in the city are increasing every year. Rents are higher now than ever before, and there is no prospect of their coming down for many years.

For it must be remembered that when we renew our building operations, which have been nearly suspended for the last four years, in consequence of the unsettled condition of the country, we shall have to provide not only for the current increase in population, but for the deficiencies which result from the past four years or more, when comparatively few houses were erected. At the present time the rent of a convenient and respectable house, suitable to the requirements of a family having a fair income, and occupying a desirable position in society, is an excessive item of cost.

And the remedy for this is to go into the country. Along the lines of our railroads and navigable waters there are localities where land is comparatively cheap,—beautiful, healthy regions, where the comforts of a rural home may be secured, with all the advantages [13] of society, and of religious and educational establishments and institutions. The facilities for reaching these country homes are already adequate for general purposes, and will be increased every year, as the demand for them grows. Railroads and steamboats are built and run for the purpose of profit on freight and passenger transportation. According to the general law of trade, the supply will equal the demand, and as the population increases along our lines of travel, the facilities and accommodations for transit will be multiplied.

Why, then, should the man who loves the country, and possesses tastes and capacities for its enjoyment, and yet is compelled by circumstances to practice economy in his mode of living, be restrained to the city limits? It is quite a practicable thing for him to realize his wishes,—live in the country and enjoy its best luxuries, without abandoning the city as far as its commercial advantages are concerned. There are localities *within an hour* of the city hall, where land can be purchased at reasonable rates, and where all the advantages of health and beauty, of retirement, pure air and attractive scenery can be enjoyed for less money than is now expended in the narrow house in the crowded street, where every sense is offended—with no open sky or distant horizon tinged with the glories of the dying day or rising morn—no grassy lawns, or waving trees, or fragrant banks of flowers. [14]

For such accommodations as he has, he pays, we will say, a rent of one thousand or twelve hundred dollars. In the country he might purchase two acres of land and build a cottage, which would afford him all, or more, conveniences than he now has, without the necessity of climbing four or five flights of stairs—at an outlay, at the usual cost of building, not exceeding six thousand dollars. The interest on this sum would be four hundred and twenty dollars. The difference between this amount and his present house rent would in a few years pay the whole cost of the place, and he would have a *home*—a centre and gathering place for his domestic interests and affections.

And this is no fancy sketch—no exaggerated statement of possibilities. We know of localities which can be reached from Wall Street in as many minutes as would be required to go to 50th Street, where land can be obtained for about five hundred dollars an acre, where there are all the conditions of health, good water, pure air, extensive and attractive views, and whatever else is desirable for a country home. In the direction we have now specially in mind, there are at least twenty railroad trains which daily stop at convenient stations, between the early morning and ten o'clock at night. For the ordinary purposes of business, and social intercourse, this is ample travelling accommodation, and as we said before, these accommodations [15] will be increased in the proportion that the country population in the neighborhood of our cities becomes more dense, and thus creates a larger demand for such facilities.

The necessity and desirableness of country homes being thus easily demonstrable, it is of importance to know how to choose sites for them, and how to build. The Poet-author of "Letters from under a bridge," has given a wise and admirable suggestion in regard to choice of sites, "leaving the climate and productiveness of soil out of the question, the main things to find united, are, *shade, water, and inequality of surface*. With these three features given by nature, any spot may be made beautiful, and at very little cost: and fortunately for purchasers in this country, most land is valued and sold with little or no reference to these or other capabilities for embellishment." There is an affluence of choice sites all over the country, and what we need most to learn is how to develop their capabilities, and add such fitting embellishments as belong to beautiful and convenient houses. Here it is that the popular taste requires additional cultivation. The impulse already given in this direction should be kept up. There is no deficiency of wealth for the appropriation and culture of these attractive places, and there is often a lavish expenditure upon country homes which ought to make them complete and even magnificent. [16] But unfortunately we see, every year, costly establishments, designed for summer residences, or for permanent homes, built up with as little regard for taste, as for expense. The deficiency is found rather in the culture than in the dispositions and means of our people. And the remedy and supply for this must be provided by the dissemination of works treating upon this and kindred topics of rural art, by means of which the public taste may be refined and elevated to a higher standard.

In constructing country houses there are several prime conditions to be observed, such as adaptation, accommodation, and expression. By adaptation is meant not only the arrangement of the main structure, as to form and material, to suit the locality and character of the grounds, but a fitness as respects the real wants—the habits and condition—of the occupants and the purposes of a country home. Nobody wants a modern city house planted down in the open country, nor should any sensible man seek a refuge from the bare streets of the city in the little less bare streets of a country village. There is no congruity between the classical forms of Grecian Architecture and the varying climate of our land.

The material used in the construction of our country houses has not been sufficiently considered by us. Timber is abundant in almost all parts of the country, [17] and the facility with which an establishment—mansion-house, office, and outbuildings—can be built up in a few weeks, of this material, has been the main reason, we suppose, why we have so many abortions, in the shape of Grecian temples, and miniature Gothic cathedrals and castles, scattered over the land. Let it be considered, that in building our country houses, we are not simply providing for ourselves, but for our children—we are constructing a homestead. It is for the want of this consideration that we have so few *homes* in our country, so few home associations, around and among which our deepest and purest affections are entwined. Our thin lath and plaster constructions, which rattle and tremble in every wind and leak in every rain, do not afford very good or permanent centers for these associations and affections.

We have some native woods that are durable, out of which we may build houses that will last for several generations; but with these, even, the cost of frequent repairs and painting is so great, to say nothing of the annoyances thereby entailed, that, in point of economy, wood is by no means the most desirable material. Nor is it, in any way, the most desirable. The prevailing taste in country dwellings, before Mr. Downing's time, was defective enough. A large, square, wooden house, painted intensely white, garnished with bright green Venetian blinds—standing [18] in a contracted yard—inclosed with a red or white wooden fence, was the very beau ideal of a gentleman's country dwelling. We are thankful that this dispensation has passed away; and we revere the memory of Downing, and of others like him, who were instrumental in bringing in a better taste in such matters.

The first cost of a stone or brick dwelling somewhat exceeds that of wood, even in places where these materials are readily obtained. But if they are properly constructed, such buildings will need very few repairs for many years. It is often objected, on the other hand, that such buildings are damp and unwholesome. This is, undoubtedly, true of many of the old stone houses which we find scattered about the country. And it is true, because they were not properly built. When properly built, they preserve the most equal temperature at all seasons. They are warm in winter and cool in summer, and the sudden changes which affect the weather without, need scarcely be felt by the delicate invalid within the walls of the stone mansion, if suitable attention is given to the simple matter of ventilation.

But let us return to the subject of adaptation. The illustrations which occur to us may serve to furnish a somewhat clear idea of what we mean by the prime conditions necessary to be observed in building.

By the term adaptation, we mean such choice of [19] style, material, size and arrangement as shall fit the structure: 1st, to the site; 2d, to the climate; and 3d, to the uses for which it is built.

And, first, as to the site: It would be obviously incongruous to erect the same house on these two different sites, with their different characteristic features and surroundings; for example, *the one* a nearly level plane gently rising, perhaps, as you approach from the road the position where the house shall stand, and sloping away again towards other broad green fields and the fertile meadows beyond—with no background of hills or mountains, no irregularly formed lake, but with a placid, lazy stream, half-sleeping, half-gliding by the weeping elms, and among the scattered groups of stately, old trees:—*the other*, a romantic hillside in the native forest, with its neighboring mountain range, where in the bright summer-time, the noisy, laughing brook keeps time to your thoughts and fancies as you wander among the hills, and in the bleak winter the winds sigh mournfully through the pines or utter their clarion calls to the spirit of the storm.

The one situation would be appropriate to the Italian villa, with its flat roof, and overhanging cornices, its spacious verandahs and balconies, all having that depth and boldness and variety of outline necessary to secure the proper effects of light and shadow [20] which, the absence of all variety of form in the landscape, would render indispensable. But no man with an artist's eye would think, for a moment, of building such a house as this on our wooded hillside. He would construct there his English cottage in good solid stone, whose steep roofs would shed with facility the summer rain and the winter snow, whose irregularities of form and outline would harmonize with nature's Gothic work in precipice and rock, in trees and climbing vines. Or else, he would place there his Swiss chalét, which would be in harmony with the scene, and a pleasing object to the eye of the observer. On the broad, open plane the villa should be made, or seem, to cover a considerable space, while the nice cottage might be built more compactly.

But here let us remark, that many of our attempts at the English cottage, generally known as the Gothic, have been failures, and some of them sad abortions.

This comes from defective models and plans, and these defects arise mainly from these sources—the lack of boldness and variety in the main outlines, and in the construction of the roofs and chimneys. Such a cottage, to be pleasing and satisfactory, must have irregularities in form, variety in ornament, and boldness in treatment. A square house with additions of gables, and dormers and pinnacles, and ridge crests, will not give us an English cottage. It is a work of [21] art, like a poem or a picture, and not a mechanical aggregation of Gothic features and ornaments. We were about to say that it should never be attempted in any other material than stone, but as many of us cannot command the means for such permanent buildings, we will concede that it may be allowable for us to put our wooden buildings into the cottage form, using the best taste and the most beautiful and picturesque styles, even if the material is objectionable.

One other observation, before we return to our main topic, may be indulged. It is simply the suggestion that too little attention has been paid to the *sky-outlines* of our country houses. Roofs and chimney-tops have been treated as necessary evils, instead of being made, as they may be, highly ornamental. The unity of the plan, as a work of art, is lost as you ascend above the eaves, all the rest seeming like excrescences growing out of structures otherwise commendable and satisfactory. The superior horizontal lines of the roof will depend somewhat upon the background of the house. When a building is placed upon the crest of a hill, or upon a slope descending from the main point of view, so that its outlines are seen against the sky, the treatment of the plan will be obviously different from that required where the background is solid, as a hill or a forest. In any case, however, the horizontal lines should be broken, as far [22] as practicable, by making the roofs of the several parts of the house of unequal height.

It will be apparent, without special argument, that our choice of style in our country houses should be controlled essentially by the climate. In our northern climate, the flat roof is objectionable, and we are obliged to modify the Italian styles somewhat in this respect, to obviate inconveniences. The hot summer sun, when, as on an August day, in the city,

"The pavements all are piping hot,
The sky above is brazen,
And every head as good as dead
The sun can shed his rays on,"

will be more than likely to open the joints and seams of the flat roof, and the sudden shower coming down with the force of a tropical storm, will find its way through, sadly to the detriment of our ceilings, our stuccoes and frescoes, as well as to the comfort and the commendable equability of temper of those who suffer the invasion. The heavy winter snows, too, require a steep roof, from which they will readily dislodge themselves without injury.

And so in the interior arrangements of the house, the provisions for heating and ventilation, for summer freedom and winter coziness, for domestic comfort and the exercise of the commendable grace of country hospitality, due regard must be had to the conditions of climate. There must be a proper adaptation to [23] them, if we would secure satisfactory country homes.

And this brings us to our last topic, the uses for which our country seats are built. The place designed simply for a summer residence for the citizen, who is obliged to be at his office or counting room daily, bating the few weeks of summer vacation, need not be so complete in its appointments and arrangements, as the permanent country residence. One essential condition, however, in this case is, that there shall be *room enough*, with ample verandahs, and shaded gravel walks, which will afford opportunities for open air exercise in all states of the weather. There is nothing, perhaps, that interferes so essentially with the citizen's enjoyment of the country, as the want of facilities for out door exercise. It is too hot or too dusty to ride or walk, before the shower, and after its refreshment has come, it is too wet and muddy. Spacious verandahs, shaded with vines, and well-made walks, always firm and dry, bordered with shrubbery, or overhung with trees, will give us "ample scope and verge enough."

But the uses of country seats depend mainly upon the tastes and habitudes of the occupants; and their adaptation in style size and arrangement should be accordingly. We believe there is no law against a man's building an elegant library and picture gallery, though he may have no taste for literature or art, but having [24] plenty of money, chooses to make this display of it. There are a great many absurdities to which poor, frail humanity is liable, against which the legislature, in its wisdom, has not thought it worth while to make solemn and positive enactments; it is better for the general moral condition of society, perhaps, that the vulgar rich man's ambition for display should manifest itself in books and pictures, rather than in fast horses. Might not the cultivation of the garden — vegetables, fruits and flowers, — take the place of both, as simple means of display? These are wholesome and agreeable employments even for those who have passed that time of life when a taste for books and art may be acquired.

A country seat should combine and express the real uses which are required by the intellectual and social condition of its occupants, and not attract attention as blazoning the wealth and money importance of the owner. If he is rich, let him make it as complete and simply elegant as he will, and this he may do without proclaiming to every passer-by his miserable pride of wealth.

With these preliminary observations, we submit our work to the judgment of those who are interested in these subjects. We have not included in our present volume any considerable number of designs for the more spacious and costly Villa, the work being [25] designed for popular use and to meet a demand which is unprovided for by previous publications.

DESIGN No. 1.

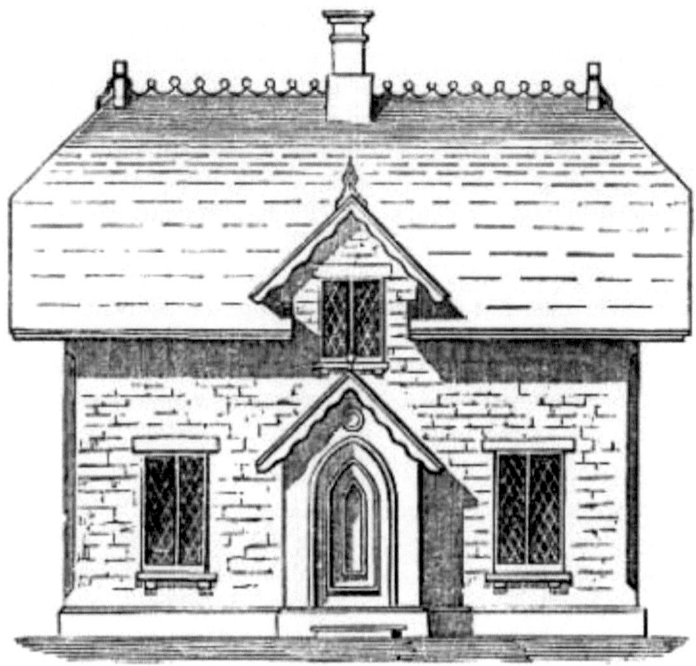

Fig. 1.—*Front Elevation.*

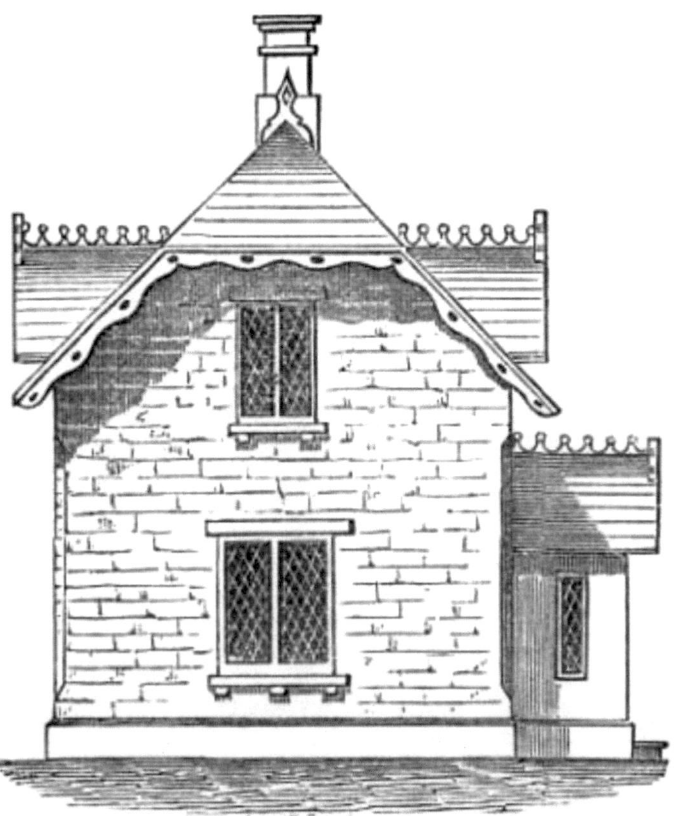

Fig. 2.—*End Elevation.*

This design as shown in figures 1 and 2, is for a laborer's cottage intended to be erected on the grounds connected with a fine estate on the western slope of the Palisades in New Jersey. It is to be built of [26] rough stone, plainly finished. It is 16 by 24 feet outside, having a living-room with bed room on the first floor, (Fig. 3,) a large pantry, stairway, etc., and a fine cellar below. The second floor (Fig. 4,) has two bed-rooms, well lighted and ventilated, and large closets to each. This size will admit of several different arrangements; the rear door might open out from the pantry, and afford more convenient access to the cellar stairs, to get in heavy articles, and shut out some cold in winter, but would interfere with the fine [27] ventilation so necessary in summer to a generally heated apartment, as a kitchen, dining, and living-room combined. A porch might be placed over the rear door, or better still, at a small additional expense, [28] a summer-kitchen and wood-house might be added. A house of this accommodation is usually the first one put up by settlers on the western prairies. They are built of wood, balloon frame, with a plain pitch roof, without ornament.

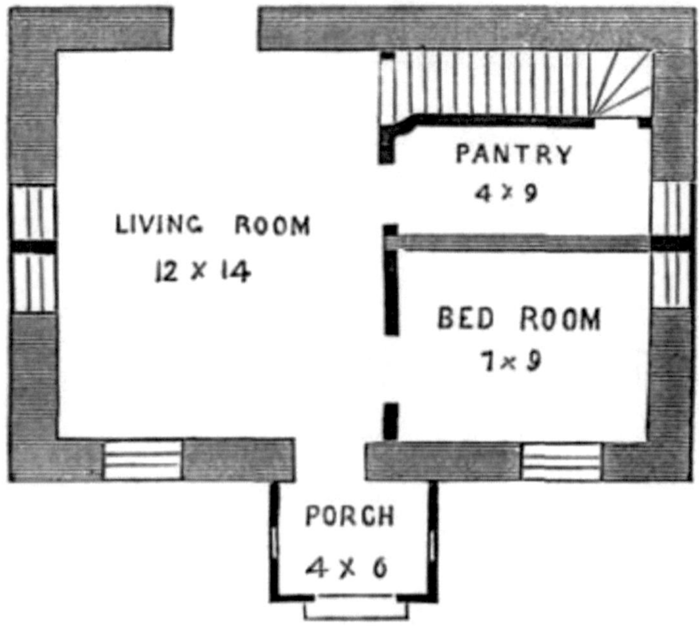

Fig. 3.—*First Floor.*

20

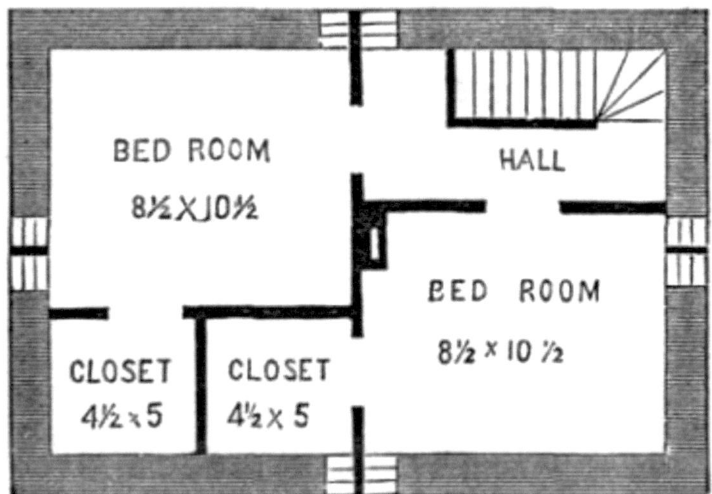

Fig. 4.—*Second Floor.*

The elevations as shown, give a greater variety than is usual in this class of building, and a house thus constructed may afterwards become a very pretty portion of a larger and more expensive structure.

DESIGN No. 2.

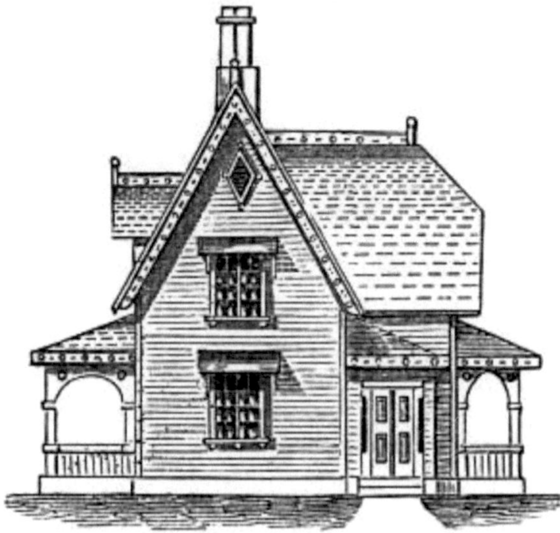

Fig. 5.—*Front Elevation.*

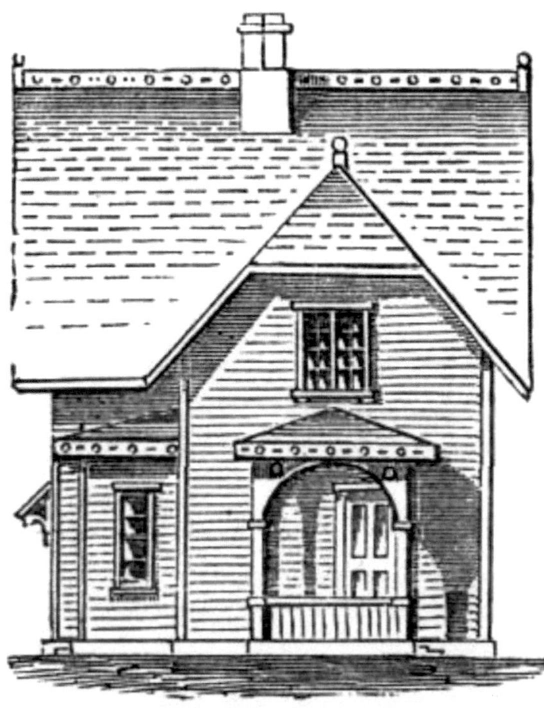

Fig. 6.—*Side Elevation.*

The second design (Fig. 5,) is for a frame building giving more variety of outline. The plan (Fig. 7,) [29] separates the sitting room from the kitchen and dining room, and insures more privacy. There is also a greater abundance of closets, though smaller. One of the bed rooms above might be divided into two, and thus increase the accommodation. A portion of the cellar may also be finished for a kitchen, and the [30] living room used as a dining room. This plan admits of future additions being made without destroying the harmony or proportion of the building. To one of moderate means, such a mode of building presents some attractions, as it affords a house for immediate wants, to which additions may be made as one's means increase. Such houses, if tastefully furnished and embellished with suitable surroundings, as neat and well-kept grounds, fine trees, shrubbery, flowers, and climbing vines, will always attract more attention and admiration than the uninviting aspect of many more expensive structures. Money tastefully expended in this manner will always yield gratifying results.

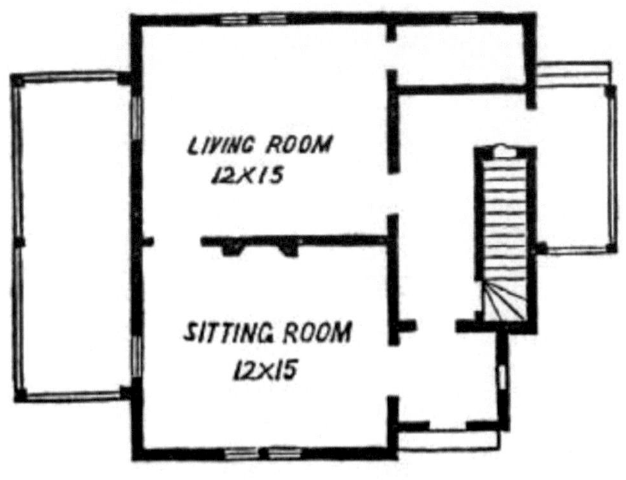

Fig. 7.—*First Floor.*

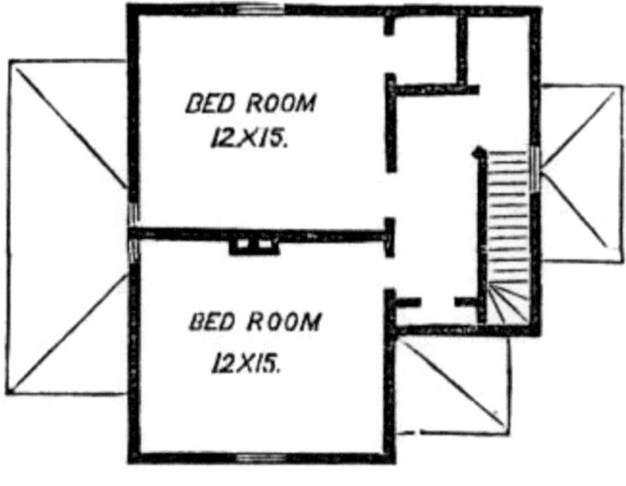

Fig. 8.—*Second Floor.*

24

DESIGN No. 3.

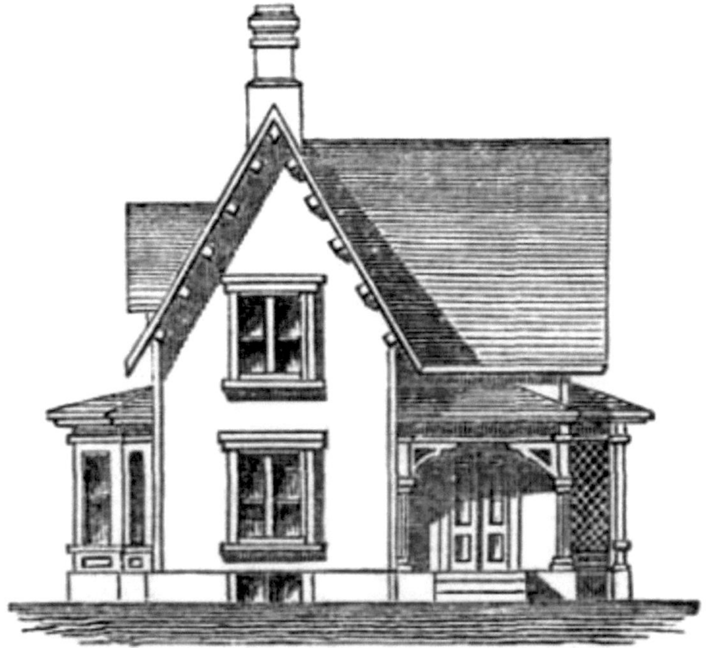

Fig. 9.—*Front Elevation.*

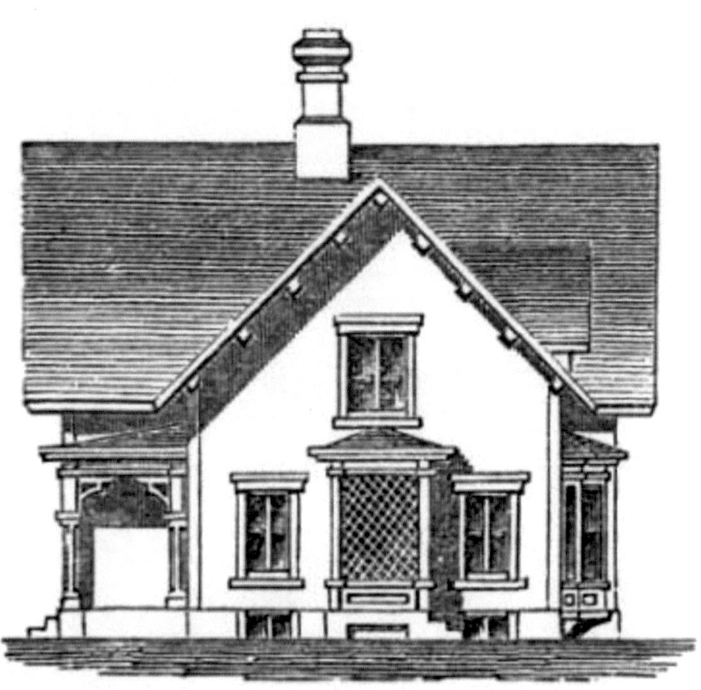

Fig. 10. — *Side Elevation.*

This design is similar, in some respects, to design No. 2, and gives, perhaps, the most compact arrangement [31] of rooms for a building having so irregular an outline. Exteriorly considered, there is much to be admired in variety, and light and shadow, the different elevations being entirely unlike each other, and [32] affording a constant change from every point of view; an object, we think, very much to be desired in cottage architecture, and when well managed never fails to make a pleasing impression. A high, bold appearance, without the overhanging eaves or depth of shadow, is not suitable for a country house; a feeling is created that something is wanting to make up the accessories of an agreeable habitation.

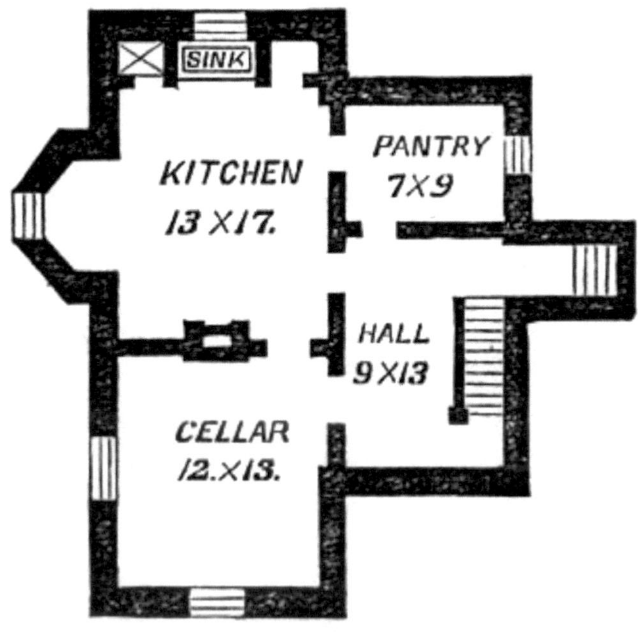

Fig. 11.—*Basement Plan.*

In this plan, (Fig. 11,) the kitchen is in the basement, convenient to the cellar, and with a good pantry attached to it. It is put there for the purpose of economizing in the construction. Our own preference is to put the kitchen in a well ventilated wing on a level with the main floor, and thus avoid, as much as possible, the necessity of running up and down stairs. This can be done at any future time when desired, as, [33] indeed, can any addition of other rooms be made to meet the wants of an increasing family. A dumb waiter connects the kitchen with the dining room, and thus saves many steps.

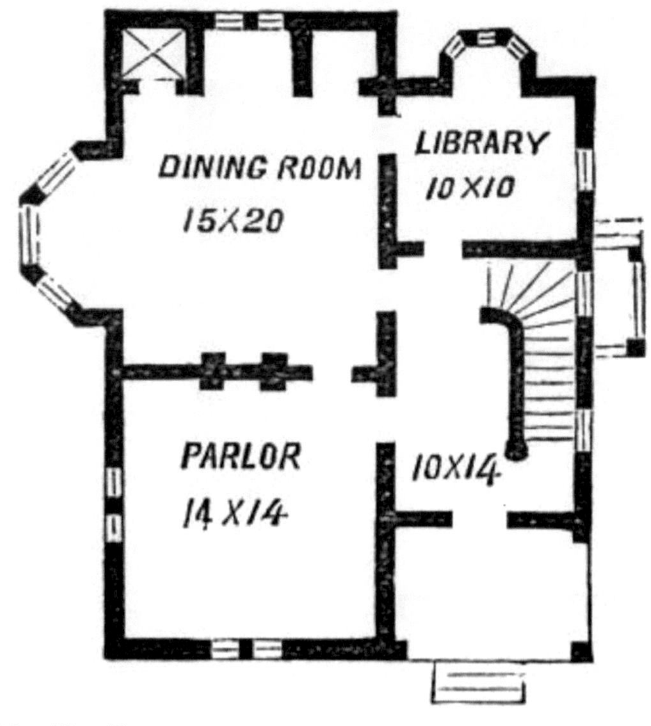

Fig. 12. — *First Floor.*

The first floor (Fig. 12,) gives parlor, dining room, and a library, with a roomy vestibule, and a side door or private entrance, and supplies all the wants of a small family. The library might be used for a bed room. On the second floor (Fig. 13,) are 3 bed rooms with closets.

The engravings are intended to tell their own story as far as possible, and but little explanation is necessary to make them fully comprehensible. In the matter of cost, one can hardly give a price that is reliable; the enormous advance in some building materials and slight advance in others, disarrange all old [34] standards of estimating. Localities, of course, have much to do with the cost; yet, above all others, the business management must be considered. A good manager, thoroughly familiar with the qualities and values of materials, who knows how to direct labor to the best advantage,

28

will execute work at a less cost than one who undertakes his own building without a previous training.

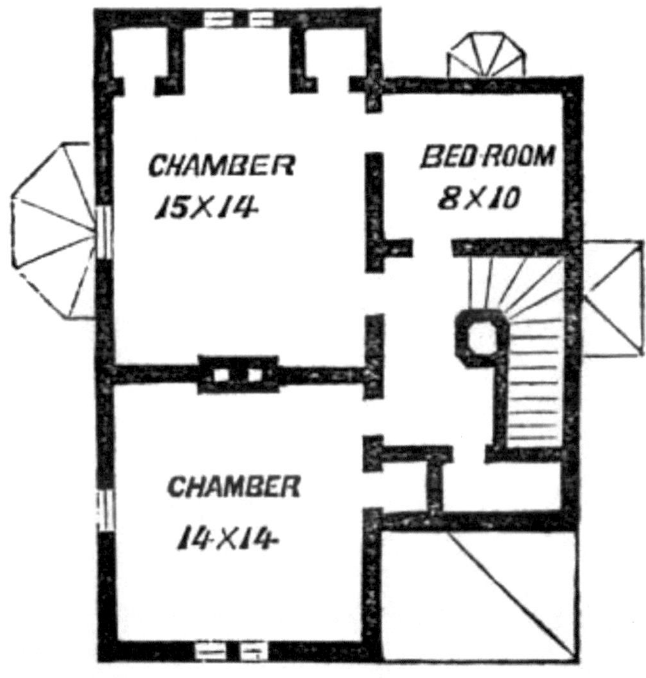

13. — *Second Floor.*

Fig.

DESIGN No. 4.

This is a perspective view of a cottage, designed to afford a reasonable amount of accommodation for an average sized family, and which, if tastefully furnished, [35] and fitted with suitable landscape surroundings, will convey a pleasing impression to all; much more so than dwellings of a more expensive class, where sufficient attention is not given to such accessories.

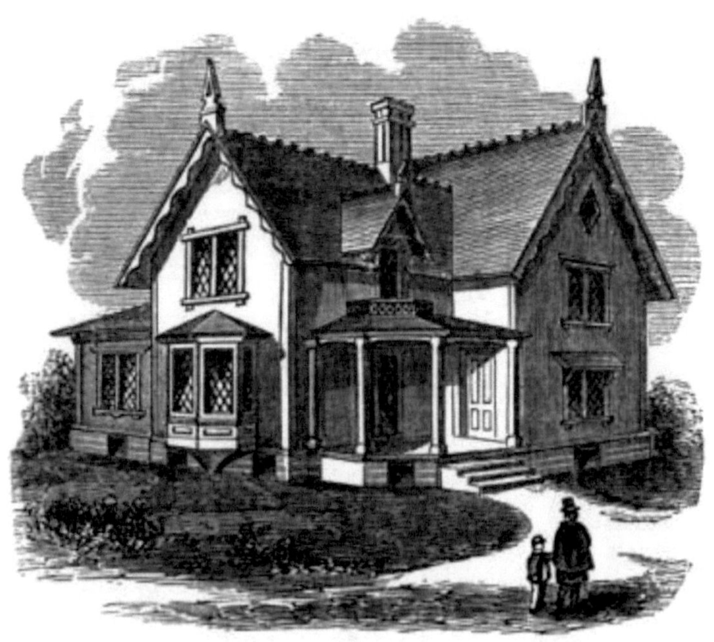

Fig. 14.—*Perspective.*

The plans of this house are compact, the rooms opening into each other in such a manner as to afford easy communication and economy in heating. The porch is spacious, and more pleasant than the long, narrow verandah. The supply of water for all purposes is from a filtering cistern, which is connected with the kitchen sink, by a pump. The entire house [36] may be heated by a furnace, hot water, or steam, as is most preferable; or stoves may be used in nearly all the rooms, if first cost is to be closely considered. A passage underneath the staircase connects with the side door from the vestibule, and, with the exception of the library, all parts of the house are accessible without passing through other rooms.

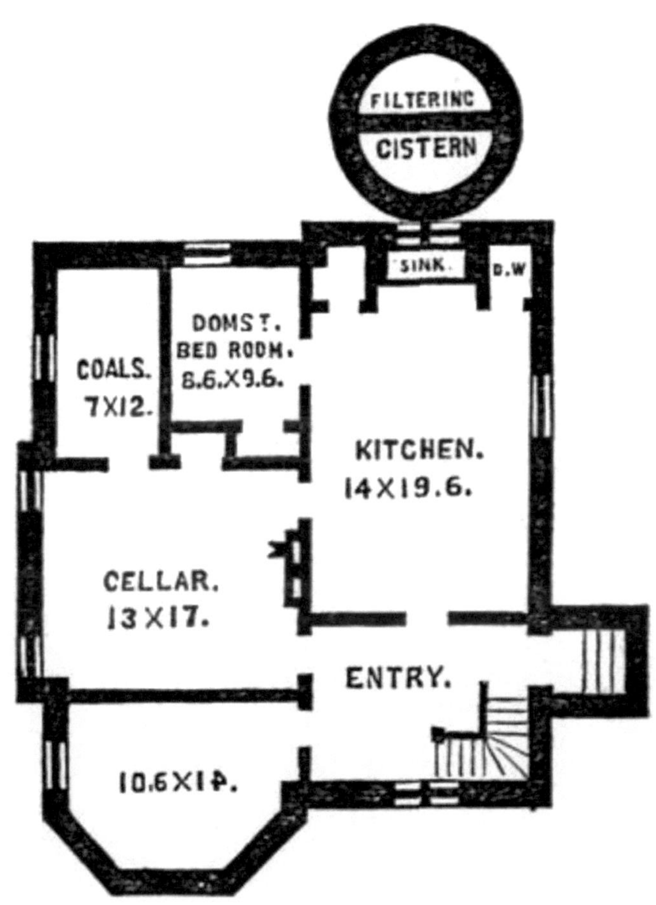

Fig. 15.—*Basement Floor.*

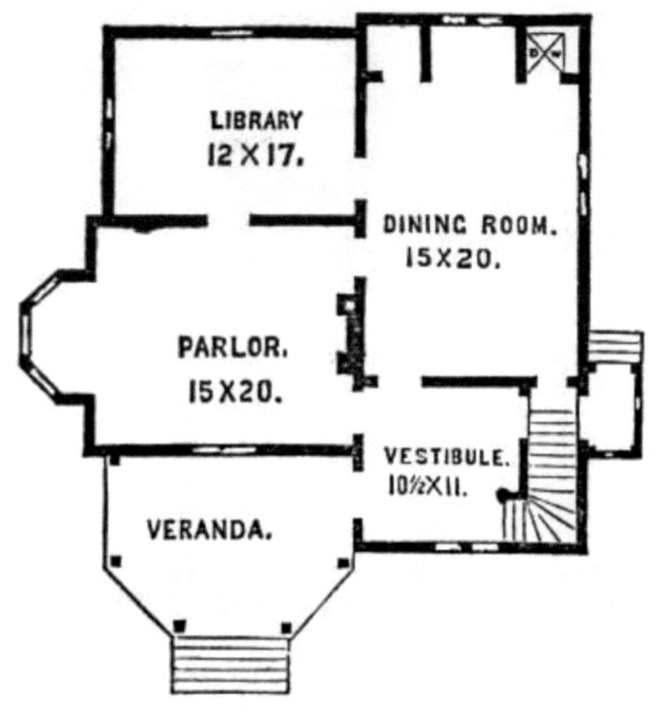

Fig. 16. — *First Floor.*

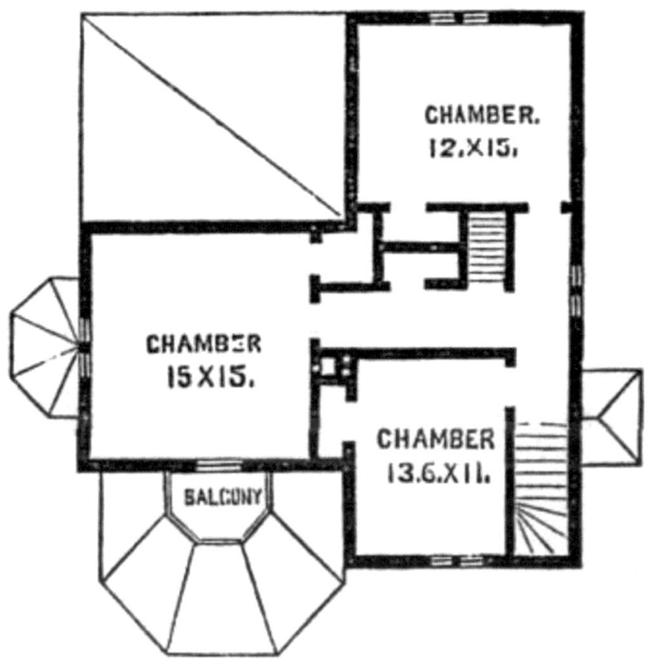

Fig. 17.—*Second Floor.*

In the vicinity of large cities, and more particularly the city of New York, there are reasons which have a money value to them, why more attention should be given to suburban architecture, and why capitalists, as well as individuals, should undertake the construction of moderate-priced buildings, that shall command attention from the harmonious combination of fine [37] architectural effects. It requires but a very limited experience to become aware of the fact, that dwellings of precisely the same cost, and similarly situated, will differ in their rental at least one half, and it is mainly owing to the reason that one is properly designed, and the other perhaps an amateur performance, modeled after the ill-proportioned Greek pediment style, too prevalent to be countenanced for a moment by any one who prides himself on his good taste. There can be no question that a fitly designed cottage, conveniently arranged, adds, independently of its own cost, a large per

33

centage to the value of the acres which surround it, and is the point which arrests the eye and secures the purchaser. Rapid rail-road facilities, lower rents, more healthful localities, and the fact [38] that the growth of this city *"Spuyten Duyvelward"* has reached a point beyond the convenient access of the strictly business man, necessarily turn the attention of those who look to the full measure of comfort, to a suburban life, ten to fifteen miles away from the unceasing noise and hurry of the city, where the business of the day is forgotten, and fresh air, fresh milk, butter and eggs, fruits, flowers, birds, &c., are luxuries unknown in town. Taking a strictly money view of building operations, for sale and rent, in suburban localities, and more particularly about New York, it would promise, by every course of reasoning, a remunerative return, if the plan were judiciously and tastefully carried out. The wants of the public, however, are so unequal, and their opinions so varied by the circumstances under which they are formed, [39] that, unless an attractive beginning can be shown, very desirable property may remain a long time on the market. If we canvass real estate thoroughly, we shall find that property sells first, and at the best prices, which has ever so humble a cottage on it, a starting point in which one may temporarily reside, and lay out his plans of future operations; for the construction of a country place is of all things one with which to make haste slowly. With those actively engaged in business, and to whom time is every thing, there is no disposition to add the labor and annoyances of building; the demand is for a home [40] ready for occupancy; the thought is entertained, and the wish gratified, simply because the opportunity presented itself; but it is far less trouble for young and middle-aged business men to stick to the city, than to give the time for building, particularly when they undertake their own architecture. Let capitalists invite them by snug, well-built, convenient, and tasteful cottages, and the demand will always be in advance of the supply, in all healthy localities, having rapid, reliable, and frequent communication with the city.

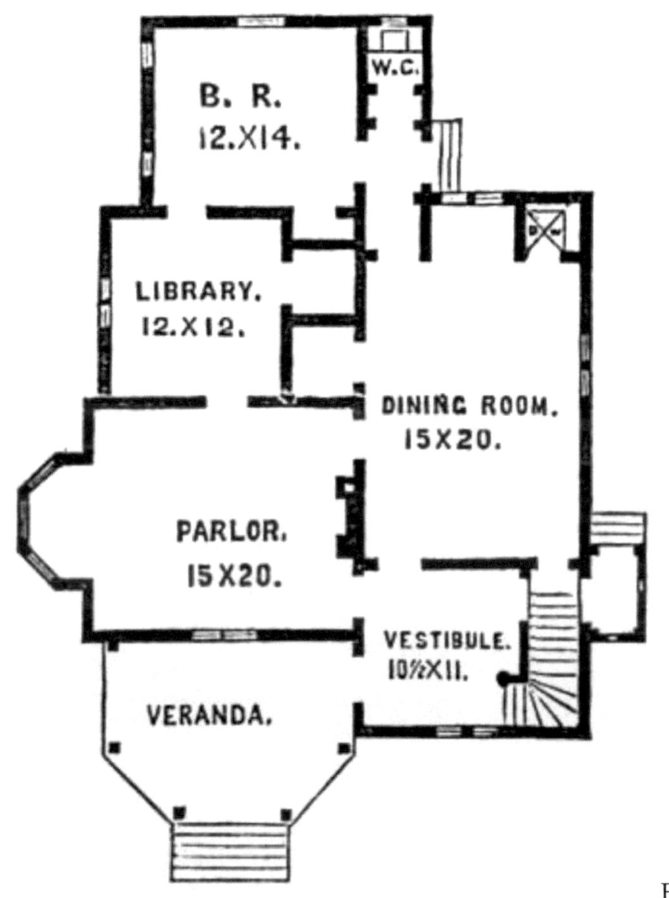

Fig. 18.—*First Floor Enlarged.*

DESIGN No. 5.

A GARDENER'S COTTAGE.

The accompanying design was made for William C. Bryant, Esq., by Fred'k S. Copley, Esq., Artist, Tompkinsville, Staten Island, and was erected on his beautiful estate at Roslyn, Long Island, in 1862. It stands on the hill above his residence, overlooking the bay from the village to the Sound, possessing one of the finest views on the Island. It was intended as a gardener's lodge, and to accommodate one or two families, as circumstances might require, (one on each floor,) giving each three rooms, and a joint right to the scullery, sink, and cellar. [41]

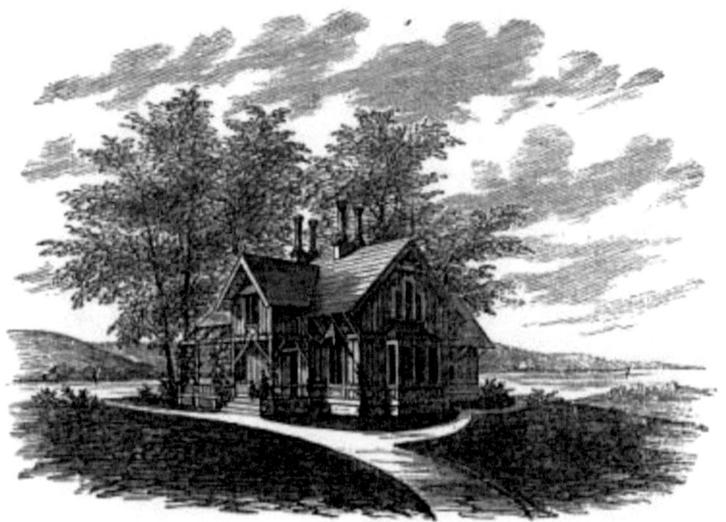

Fig. 19. — *Perspective View.*

[42]

Arrangement. — The first story is 9 feet in the clear throughout, with every convenience suitable for the health and comfort of the occupants. From the porch, a small hall, lighted from the roof, is entered, with doors on either hand, to parlor or living room, and staircase passage in front, communicating with the kitchen at the back, chambers above, and cellar beneath.

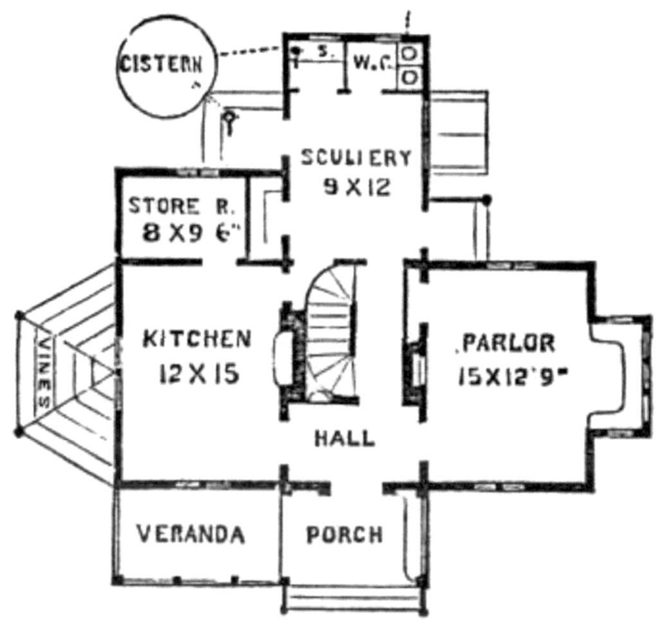

Fig. 20. — First Floor.

The chamber floor, second story, is 9 feet in the clear through the centre, and 6 feet at the sides, (from the floor to the plate,) the roof cutting off three feet of the ceiling at the sides at an angle of 45 degrees. This loss of a few feet of the ceiling is more than compensated by the cottage-like effect it gives to the rooms, harmonizing the inside with the external appearance. The two principal chambers are provided [43] with fire-places and ample closet room. The one over the parlor has two closets, built outside the frame, and a door into the single room, over the porch, forming a most desirable family chamber. Both these rooms have ventilators in the same chimney breast, and the small one may be warmed by a stove leading thereto. The other has a large closet over the store-room for trunks, linen, &c. The attic room over the kitchen wing is intended for the domestics.

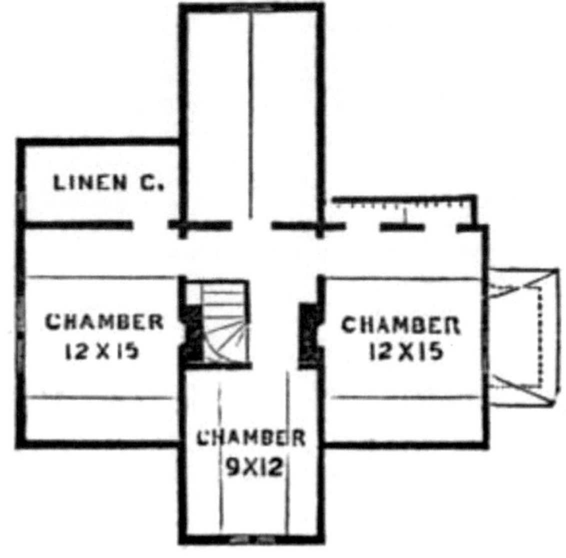

Fig. 21.—

Chamber Floor.

By reference to the plans, it will be seen that every room is of good size and form, cheerfully lighted, thoroughly ventilated, and of easy access one to another, at the same time that privacy, so essential, is maintained throughout.

Construction.—The building is constructed of wood, vertically sided, and battened, (with 1½ inch tongued and grooved pine plank,) with horizontal strips in [44] line of the window sills and floors, to hide the buts, and small triangular pieces in the corners, which gives the pretty effect of paneling. The whole is stained by a mixture of oil, &c., that heightens the grain of the wood, and gives a brightness of color, and that cheerfulness of effect, so desirable in rural dwellings. The roof is of slate, in bands of purple and green, and the chimneys are surmounted by terra-cotta pots. The whole is filled in with brick.

This cottage is built in a substantial and plain manner, with cellar under kitchen, cemented on the gravel the same as the cistern, and all the interior wood work is oiled and stained.

As a specimen of cottage architecture, (on the smallest scale, lodge class,) it will rank as one of the best. For simplicity, variety of form, symmetry of proportion, with convenience of arrangement and economy of space and construction, it forms a model cottage, that any one might live in and many covet, besides being an addition to the landscape and an ornament to the grounds.

[45]

DESIGN No. 6.

STONE STABLE AND COACH HOUSE.

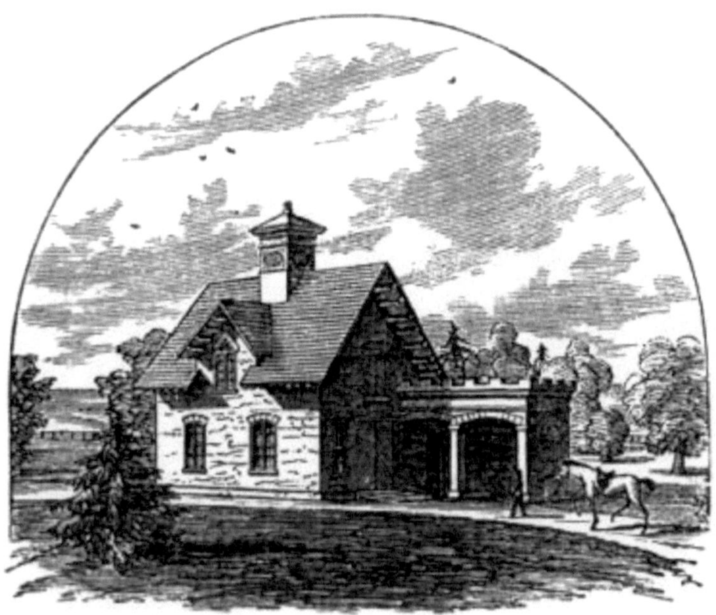

Fig. 22.—*Perspective.*

This design was erected on the Hudson, during the past year, of the beautiful rock faced stone so abundant between the Spuyten Duyvil and the Highlands, and is a good example of such a building as will meet the requirements of a moderately extensive establishment. It is conveniently arranged, enabling all the work to be done with the most ease, and gives thorough light and ventilation, so essential to the health and comfort of animals. The time has gone by to give prospective prices for anything, but we have seen the day [46] when this building might have been erected for about $4,000. A room for the coachman may easily be made on the second floor, and the plan increased or decreased to suit the wants of any one.

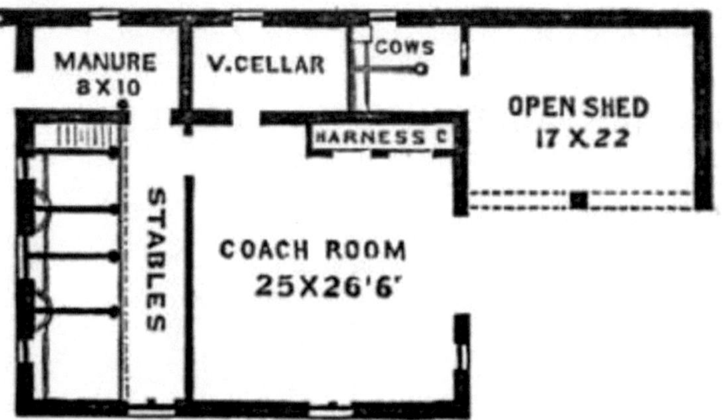

Fig. 23.—*Ground Plan.*

DESIGN No. 7.

A FARM COTTAGE.

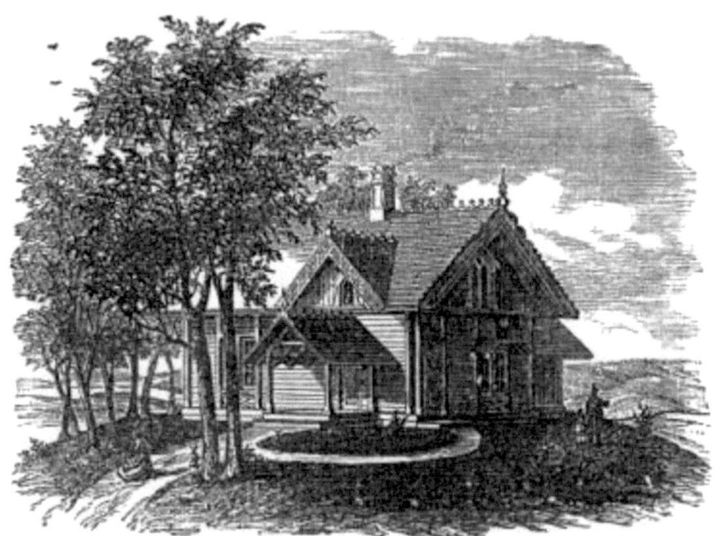

Fig. 24.—Perspective View.

We show in this design a style of cottage which, in these high priced times of lumber and labor, can be erected at a very reasonable figure; and although prepared for a farm cottage, will admit of such changes as will adapt it to the wants of those who require a higher grade of accommodation. It is the most natural thing in the world for any one to take up a plan and suggest innumerable changes and additions, always forgetting the unalterable condition of price, situation, and object, [48] [47] which restrained the architect while working it up. To prepare a design regardless of expense is a very different matter from devising one that gives the largest amount of accommodation within a fixed limit of cost. We shall arrive gradually at the precise figures, and endeavor to get the accommodation wanted by some of our readers.

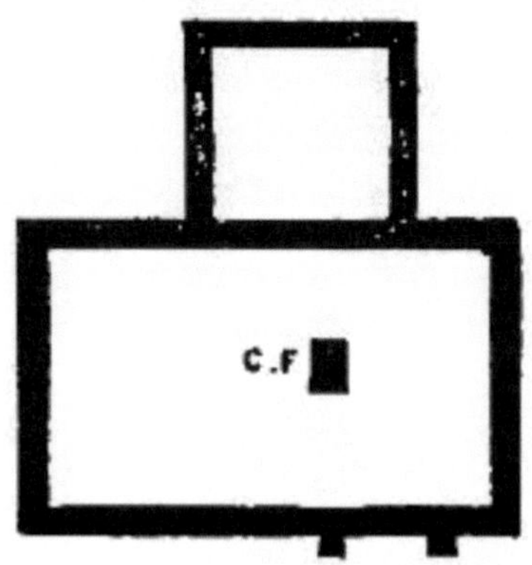

Fig. 25. — *Cellar.*

Fig. 26. — First Floor.

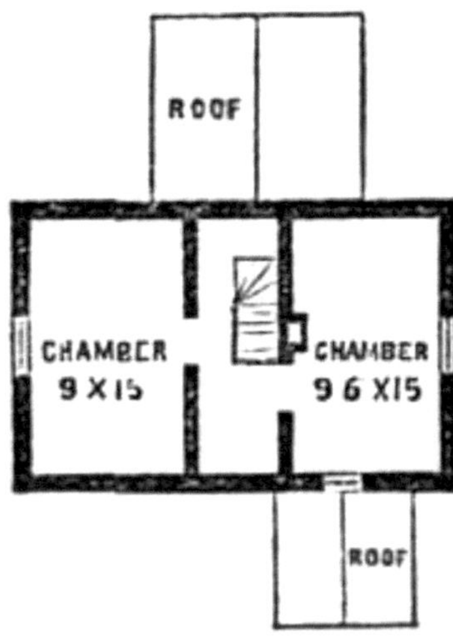

Fig. 27.—Second Floor.

It has been frequently observed that the gate lodges and farm cottages attached to large estates are generally more attractive in their architectural proportions and beauty than the mansion itself; and this has been usually attributed to the education of the proprietor's tastes, the cottages being the latest erections. This impression is not, however, always true; for there is a peculiar beauty and attractiveness about cottage architecture which can not be produced in buildings of a larger and more commodious class. Certain it is that a prettily designed cottage will always arrest attention. "Among the first and most [49] pleasing impressions," says a late writer, "of our trite friend, the intelligent foreigner, as he entered England by the old Dover road, were those suggested by the little whitewashed and woodbined cottages which caught his eye at every turn. All books of travels on English ground are full of them. Snugly sheltered in its bower of apple trees, or more stately group of walnuts, approachable only by its rustic stairs, or dotted at neighborly distances along the straggling village, with its trim garden of lavender and wall flowers, seen through the wicket gate or over the privet hedge, the English cottage, above or below, near or in the distance, was alike the delight and envy of the traveler, the theme of the journalist and the poet. 'There is scarce a cottage,' says an American tourist just landed from America and France, 'between Dover and London which a poet might not be happy to live in. I saw a hundred little spots I coveted with quite a [50] heart-ache.' Whether or not Rogers would have given up his picture-lighted snuggery in St. James' Place for his 'Cot beside the hill,' and really preferred to have his latch lifted by the pilgrim, instead of his knocker by a London footman, it is certain that the cottage homes of England that border the main roads have long possessed a beauty far beyond the houses in other lands belonging to classes much higher in the social scale, and have been coveted, sometimes not without reason, by those who could, if they chose, have purchased them fifty times over."

DESIGN No. 8.

This design for a timber cottage is simple and at the same time picturesque, and built upon a site adapted to it, and in harmony with the architectural expression, the effect could not fail to be in a high degree pleasing.

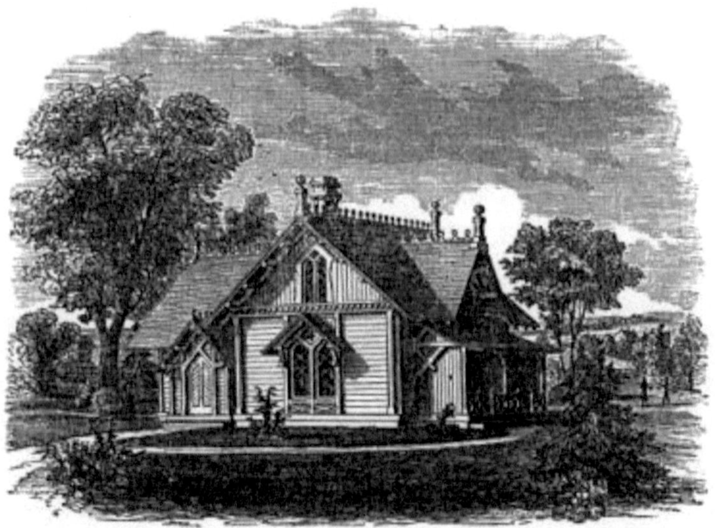

Fig. 28. — Perspective View.

It will be seen that some of the principal timbers of the frame are intended to show on the outside, and that there is a designed contrast between the horizontal siding extending to the top of the posts, and the vertical and battened covering of the pediment above the ornamental string course. The brackets and posts [52] [51] which support the roof of the porches, should be chamfered, and these timbers should be of sufficient thickness to avoid any appearance of meanness, while at the same time, they should not be too heavy, and so destroy the proportions of the design.

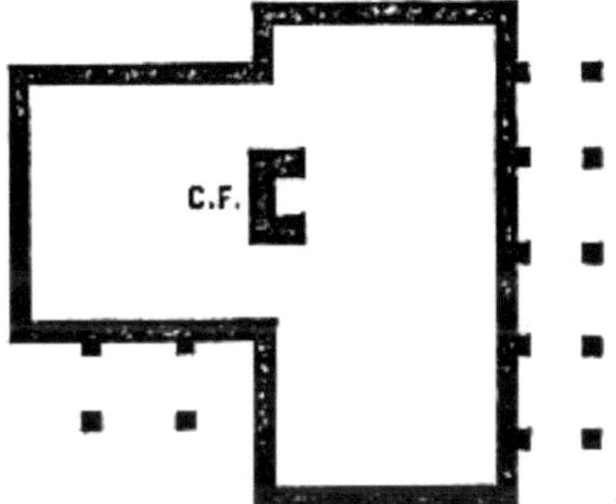

Fig. 29. — Cellar.

The roof should be covered with shingles having their ends clipped or rounded.

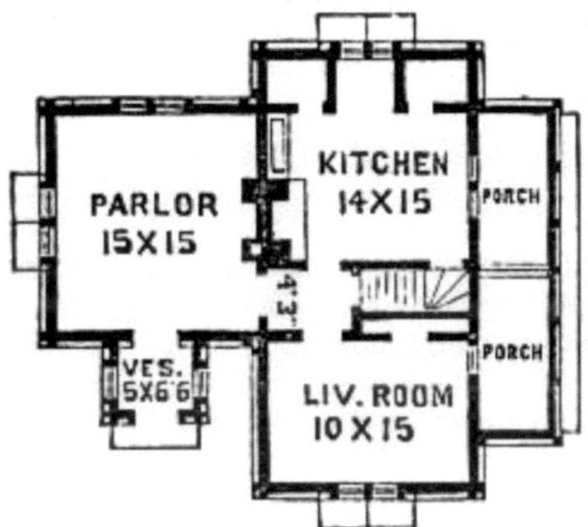

Fig. 30. — First Floor.

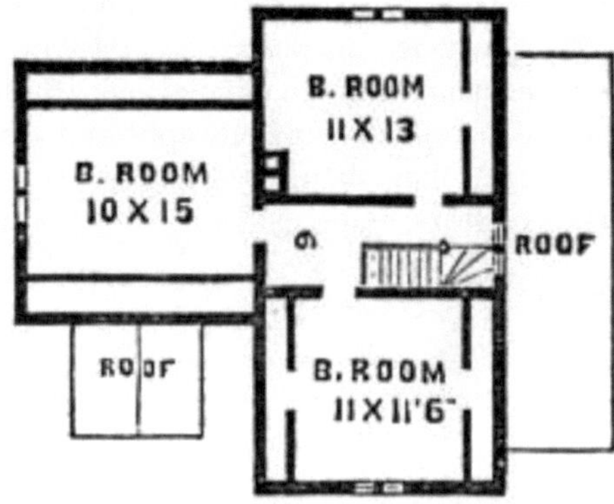

Fig. 31.—Second Floor.

The cellar may be divided in such way as to serve the wants of the occupants. A portable furnace might be placed at the foot of the basement stairs, which [53] would warm the rooms on the first floor, and temper the air of the chambers above.

The interior accommodations and conveniences are readily seen on inspection of the plans—(Figs. 30. 31). There is no waste of room, and for the uses of a small family, the accommodations would be found as ample as could well be obtained in a cottage of such size and cost.

DESIGN No. 9.—RURAL CHURCH.

DESIGNED BY THE REV. DR. CRESSY.

This design is intended for a church which is to occupy a beautiful and commanding site on the western shore of Lake George, in the midst of the original forest, and is now in process of erection. It will also meet the requirements of several correspondents who have requested plans for rural churches which could be erected as economically and cheaply as possible, with due regard to proportion, fitness and beauty of expression.

This design will be found to comprehend, we may say, in an eminent degree, variety of outline, correctness of detail, force of expression and purity of taste, with simplicity of execution, and in those parts of the [54] country where lumber is abundant, and labor not exorbitant, it can be erected at a low cost.

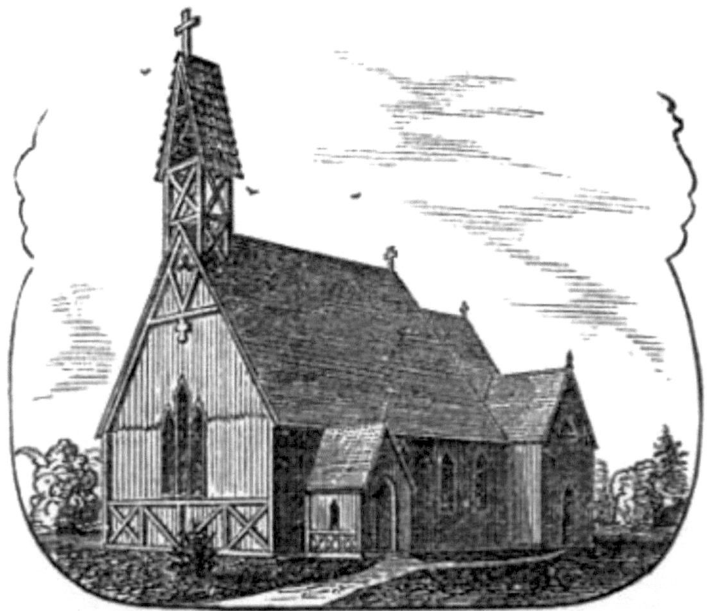

Fig. 32.—*Perspective.*

We have a right to congratulate ourselves on the improvement which the last quarter of a century has witnessed among our people in the building and adorning of our edifices devoted to Christian worship. Downing, in his time, said, "that the ugliest church architecture in Christendom, is at this moment to be found in the country towns and villages of the United States." And speaking of the influence of what our churches should be, in the beauty of their proportions, and in the expression of the sacred purposes which they embody, and the feelings of reverence and harmony with God and man which they suggest, he fitly says—"We fear there are very few country churches in our land that exert this kind of spell,—a spell [55] which grows out of making stone, and brick, and timber, obey the will of the living soul, and express a religious sentiment. Most persons, most committees, select men, vestrymen, and congregations, who have to do with the building of churches, appear indeed wholly to ignore the fact, that the form and feature of a building may be made to express religious, civil, domestic, or a dozen other feelings, as distinctly as the form and features of the human face: — and yet this is a fact as well known by all true architects, as that joy and sorrow, pleasure and pain, are capable of irradiating or darkening the countenance. Yes, and we do not say too much, when we add, that right expression in a building for religious purposes, has as much to do with awakening devotional feelings, and begetting an attachment in the heart, as the unmistakable signs of virtue and benevolence in our fellow-creatures have in awakening kindred feelings in our own breasts.

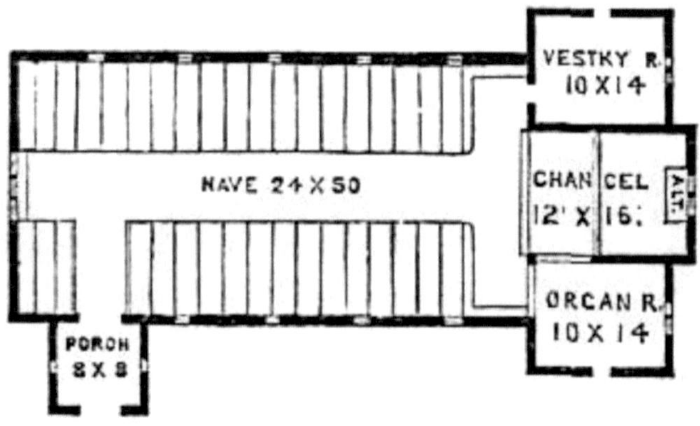

Fig. 33. — *Floor Plan.*

[56]

"We do not, of course, mean to say that a beautiful rural church will make all the population about it devotional, any more than that sunshine will banish gloom; but it is one of the influences that prepare the way for religious feeling, and which we are as unwise to neglect, as we should be to abjure the world and bury ourselves, like the ancient troglodytes, in caves and caverns."

Happily we are coming to appreciate these truths, not only in our cities, but in the country, and the ugly, unsightly, and unseemly structures which have so long deformed the land are giving place to edifices in which the true ideas of harmony, grace, proportion,

48

symmetry and expression, which make what we call Beauty, are brought out in due proportion.

The church we present is designed to be of wood, the country about the site affording an abundance of that material, at the lowest cost. An inspection of the design will show that the principal timbers of the frame are intended to be visible externally,—the weather-boarding being set back from the face of the posts and beams. This exterior covering is intended to be made of sound *rough* plank, from ten to fourteen inches wide, and at least one and a-half inches thick. These are to be tongued and grooved, so as to make a close joint, and nailed to the frame in a *vertical* manner. The joint is to be covered with a narrow [57] strip, or batten, of one and a-half inch plank. These unplaned plank may be painted with two good coats and sanded, or they may be left to take such tints and complexion as time and the weather may give them.

Lumber, at the proposed site, being cheaper and more easily obtained than lime, the interior of the church will be neatly ceiled with narrow boards, which will be lightly stained and oiled. The roof will be "open timber" of simple construction. All the wood work of the interior will be of pine, smoothly planed, stained and oiled, without paint, except the ceiling of the roof which should be colored, in order to give something like warmth of tone to the interior, the lack of which is often sadly felt in our country churches, particularly.

This mode of weather-boarding and "open timber" finish is now so common that a more particular description is unnecessary.

This church will seat, comfortably, about two hundred persons. Its cost will depend entirely upon the price of lumber and labor, of course, and these vary with different localities, and are particularly uncertain at this time. We will only add that it will cost no more to build with correct proportions and in good taste, than in disregard and defiance of these desirable and commendable principles.

[58]

DESIGN No. 10.

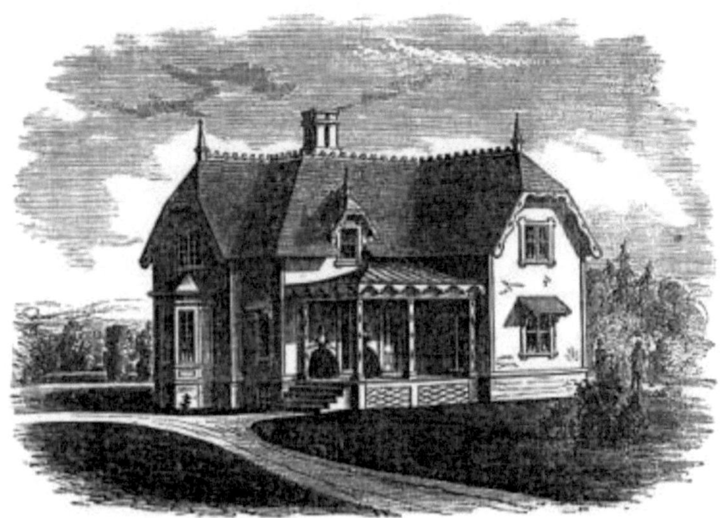

Fig. 34.—*Perspective.*

We give below a somewhat different example of Cottage Architecture, of a form that is compact and every way available, at the same time affording every convenience in the arrangement of rooms desirable for a family of refined tastes and moderate means. This cottage may be built of wood, or, better still, in favorable localities, of brick or stone, and if suitably surrounded with tasteful landscape embellishments, will make a snug, pretty, and attractive home. One can, by the exercise of appropriate taste, produce the right kind of an impression in a house of this character. It should become a part of, and belong to the acres which surround it; it should be an indispensable accessory to the place itself, and the grounds should be laid out and embellished in such a manner that the whole combination impresses all with harmonious beauty, and not, as is too frequently the case, seek to make up the wretched deficiencies in the grounds by elaborate expenditure and display about the house. A true appreciation of country life will not tolerate slovenly, ill-kept grounds, and no house exhibits its true value unless there is a harmony in its surroundings. If this be attended to, a high degree of effect can be produced in houses of very moderate cost; [60] [59]

houses that shall be roomy, warm, substantial, and in every way agreeable to their occupants.

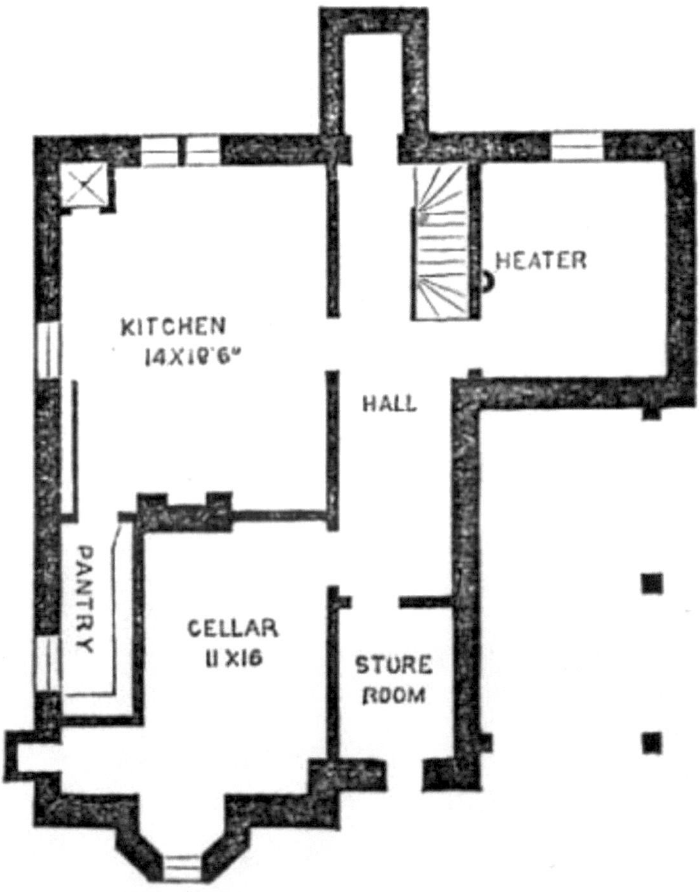

Fig. 35.—*Basement Plan.*

The plans show the arrangement of rooms, and these can be made larger or smaller, or be differently disposed, to suit almost any fancy. In this design the kitchen apartments are below stairs; in future plans we shall give some with kitchen, laundry, etc., on the principal floor; or they can be readily added to this plan. The cost of a house is the one thing desirable; every one asks for it, and yet every one within our knowledge who has built a house himself at a stated price has been sadly deceived. Close [61] specifications are very dry reading, and not appropriate here, and it is questionable how much service they would be to any but professional builders. It is reasonable to suppose, that if one without building experience undertakes it, he will have to pay something additional for the knowledge he will gain. If he places it to the proper account, then we can not be accused of misleading him.

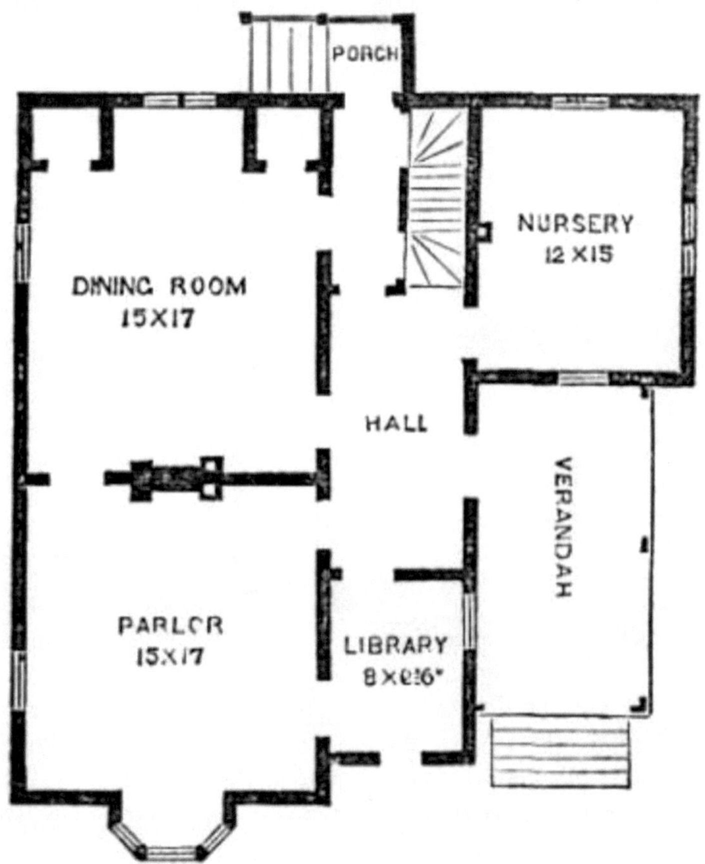

Fig. 36.—*First Floor.*

52

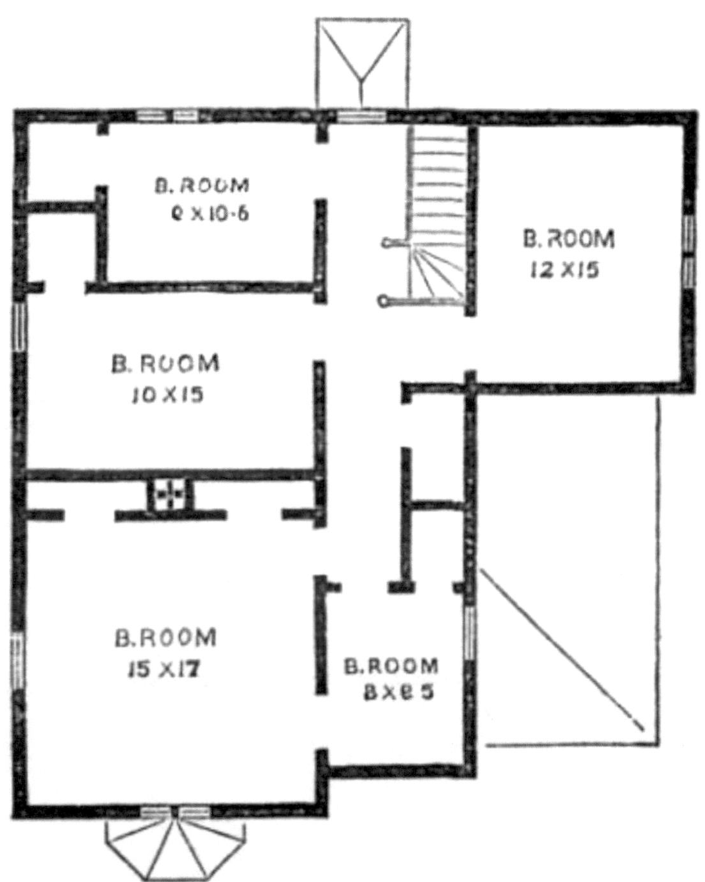

Fig. 37. — *Second Floor.*

Most men contemplate, at some period of life, the construction of a dwelling-house, but few deem it necessary to study their wants or prepare their plans until they have selected their site and made all other [62] arrangements for building, and then proceed with all possible haste to plan a home. That which should have been the study of months or years, is hurried through in as many days, imperfectly done at the best, and the cause of frequent annoying and expensive changes after the work has commenced. It is true, that the site has very much to do with the distribution of rooms, but any ingenious architect can readily adapt a proper combination of rooms to suit the exposures and views of a particular site. It would be vastly better for those who prefer to arrange their own plan of rooms, (and there are but very few who do [63] not,) that they take abundant time to consider well every thing relating to them; and although the hope of building may be very remote, it should not be considered time lost to begin to give one's thoughts a definite form of what he thinks a house should be; for if nothing else results, it may furnish a valuable hint for a friend, and will certainly enlarge one's information and experience in these matters. Almost every one is capable, with such hints as have been freely given in the volumes of the Horticulturist, in the leading papers which treat on rural art, and the numerous valuable publications on rural architecture, to make such a combination of rooms as will best suit his peculiar wants, tastes, or fancies, and then, with the aid of an architect, it can readily be freed from mechanical impracticabilities, and put into a proportionate and harmonious form. Architecture, both in design and construction, is a profession that requires long years of study and practice to develop an expert, and those who really want a good thing at the least cost, usually seek such assistance; those who prefer to do their own designing and building, find out with absolute certainty the most expensive modes of erecting very ugly and ill-proportioned structures.

[64]

DESIGN No. 11.

A SUBURBAN SUMMER HOUSE.

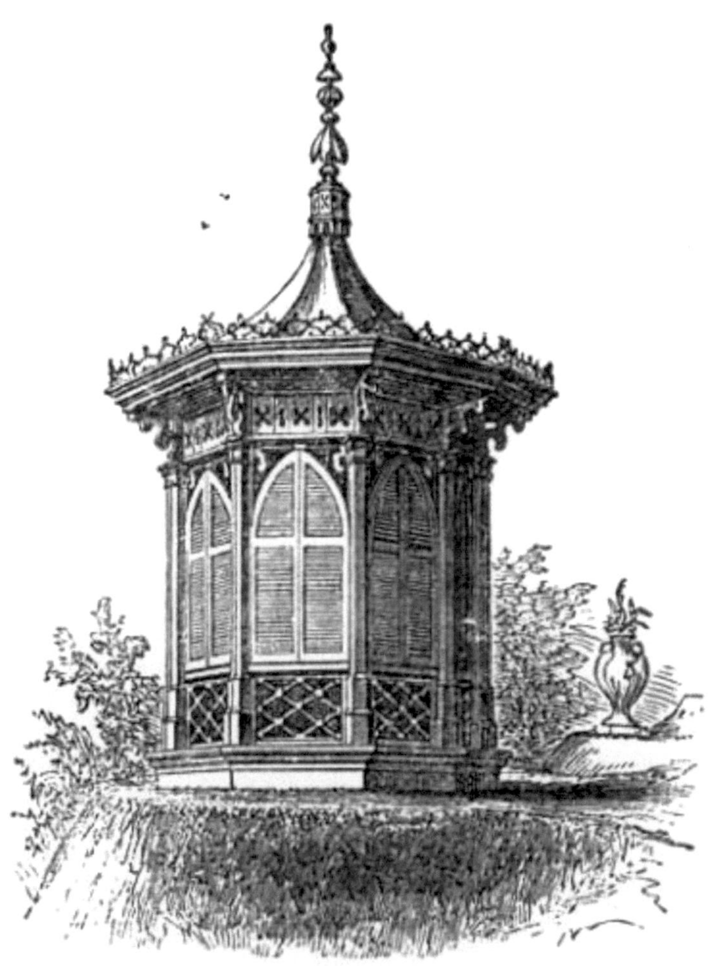

Fig. 38.

In the adornment of ornamental grounds, some considerable attention has been given to summer houses, and similar structures; but these have been mainly *rustic* in their design and finish, and in this respect well adapted to their purpose and surroundings. The good taste of these structures will not be called in question. There are locations, however, in the more immediate vicinity of our large cities, where a style [65] less rustic would seem to be more in harmony with the architecture which is found to prevail. We refer to residences on the outskirts of our large cities, with inclosures containing a few city lots. Here the architecture, so far from being rural, is, on the contrary, stiff, sharp, and sometimes very ornate. A rustic summer house in such a place would be an incongruity. A rustic house is in itself a beautiful object; but there is a certain charm in association which can not be widely departed from without doing violence to our conceptions of the fitness of things; and hence a purely rustic house without rural surroundings is destitute of the chief elements which give rise to the beautiful. Most persons would say it was out of place.

The design herewith presented was prepared to meet the requirements of such a case; it is consequently somewhat elaborate. It is located on a small plot of ground within the city limits, and in full view from three streets. The grounds are laid out with a few rectangular walks, and such shrubs as the small size of the place would admit of. The house, we think corresponds with its surroundings. Its faults, if any, are a little too much ornament, but something of this kind seemed to be required in the absence of that more beautiful ornamentation produced by the drapery of Nature. The house is so located that it receives the morning sun for a few hours, but during the [66] rest of the day is in the shade; it therefore constitutes a pleasant place of retreat for the family at all hours, and is used by the children freely as a play house. The floor is laid in narrow stuff, and is elevated a foot above the ground for the sake of dryness. Easy seats, a handsome centre table, and a hanging lamp complete the interior. Venetian blinds afford ample protection on a misty day or a chilly night, or admit the soft summer breeze on a hot and sultry eve. — *Horticulturist.*

DESIGN No. 12.

STABLE AND CARRIAGE HOUSE.

This stable affords abundant accommodation for three horses, with carriage house, feed room, and a large harness room on the first floor, while the loft above may contain a coachman's room, and leave ample space for hay and straw.

If required, a shed and cow house can be extended on the side opposite the carriage house, thus adding considerably to the effect of the external appearance. Under the stable there should be a cellar for the storage of roots for feed, and, if desirable, the winter stock of vegetables for household use. This stable may be built of wood, or of stone or brick. [67]

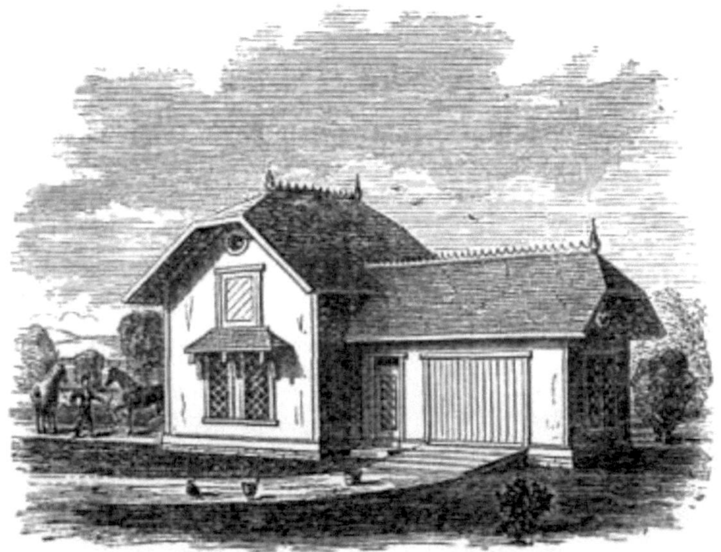

Fig. 39. — *Stable.*

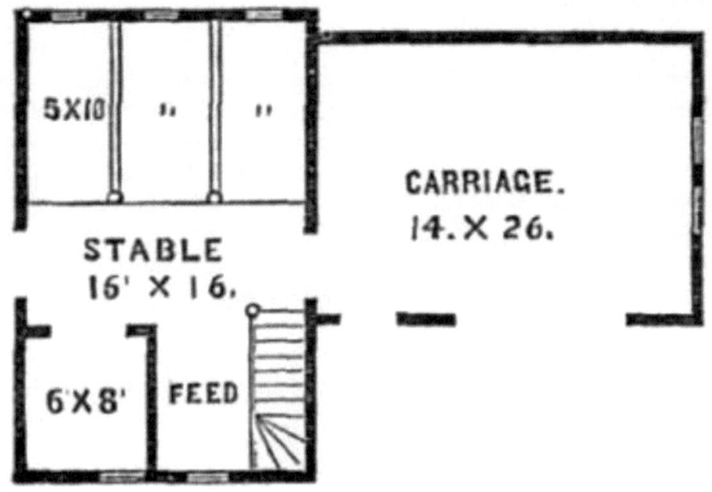

Fig. 40.—*Stable Plan.*

[68]

DESIGN No. 13.

This design is intended to cover, at a low cost, as much comfort and convenience as a moderate-sized family would require, and to distribute the same as much as possible on one floor.

The cellar or basement kitchen is dispensed with and only enough cellar room provided to meet the wants of those who occupy suburban places of a few acres in extent. Where large quantities of vegetables are stored, or where cellar room is required for farm purposes, we think it better to build cellars separate from the residence, (an arrangement much more healthful, as well as convenient and desirable.) For the preservation in warm weather of meats, milk, and other perishable articles, a refrigerator, or, better still, an ice closet, can be set up at one end of the laundry. This can be supplied with ice through an outside door, and is infinitely better and more convenient than any cellar or spring house.

The kitchen is without a fire-place, but is provided with a ventilator in the chimney near the ceiling. The cooking may be done by a stove, which, if properly contrived, is one of the most effective ven-

tilators, and preferred by many housekeepers for all kitchen purposes. Or a range can be placed in the chimney, if [70] [69] desirable,
or a fire-place, if it should be considered indispensable.

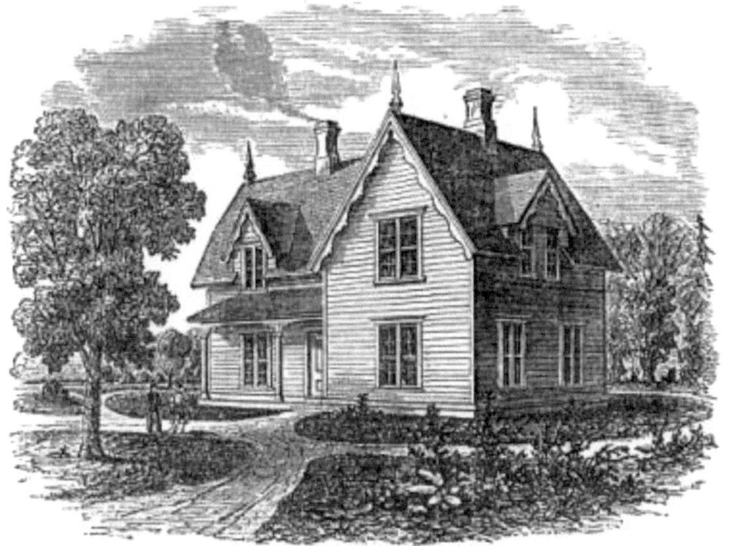

Fig. 41.—*Elevation.*

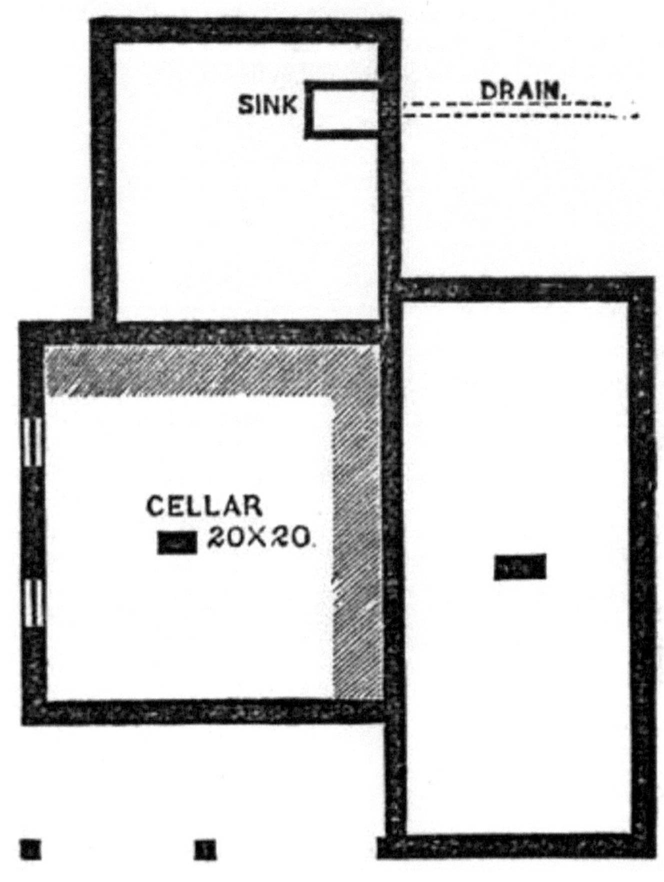

Fig. 42.—*Plan.*

A door under the stair-way separates the front and rear halls, and disconnects the kitchen apartments from the rest of the house. All the doors opening into the rear hall should be hung with the new spiral spring butt, the best door spring that has come under our notice. It is entirely concealed, and works without a fault.

The closets in the dining room are finished to give an interior appearance of a bay window. The dining room and the two chambers above, are intended to be heated by a fire-place heater set in the chimney, thus [71] warming three rooms, at pleasure, with one fire.

60

A small stove in the library will keep that comfortable. Or, in place
of all this, the whole house may be heated by any of the approved
modes, in the use of hot air, hot water, or steam.

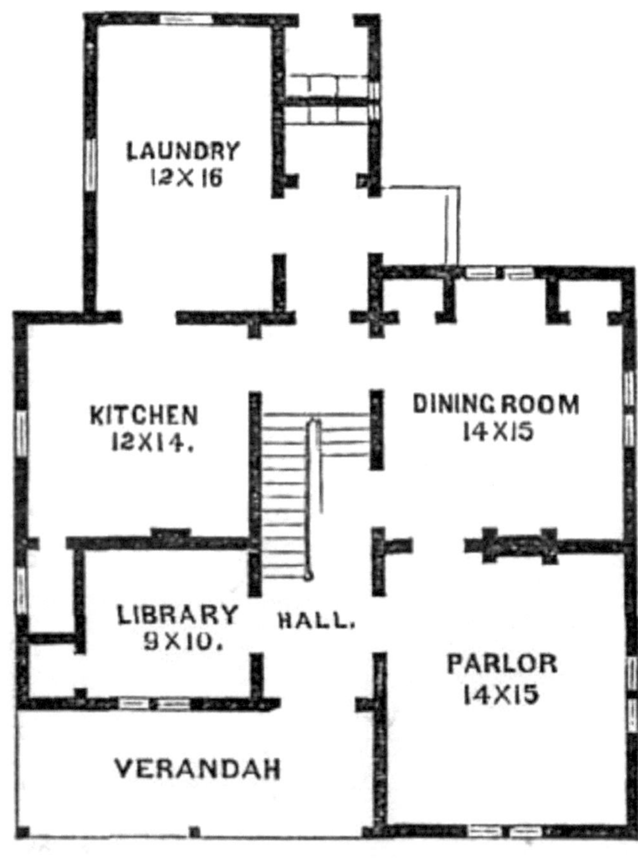

Fig.
43. — *First Floor.*

The library, parlor, or general living room in a country house —
and we like these rooms in one — should have the cheerful, healthful
luxury of an open fire-place, and we know of no more elegant,
cleanly and effective contrivance for this purpose than Dixon's low
down, Philadelphia Grate, in which wood, coal, or any other fuel
can be used equally well. The advantages [72] combined in this

grate are these:—the fire flat on the hearth, and radiating the heat from an oval cast iron backing: cold air supplied from below, and ashes, dirt, &c., shaken down into an ash-pit in the cellar, beneath the grate. We speak confidently of this invention, after a trial of two winters, and do not hesitate to say that, compared with this, the ordinary grate is worthless. Large rooms can be kept perfectly comfortable in the coldest weather, without heat from any other source.

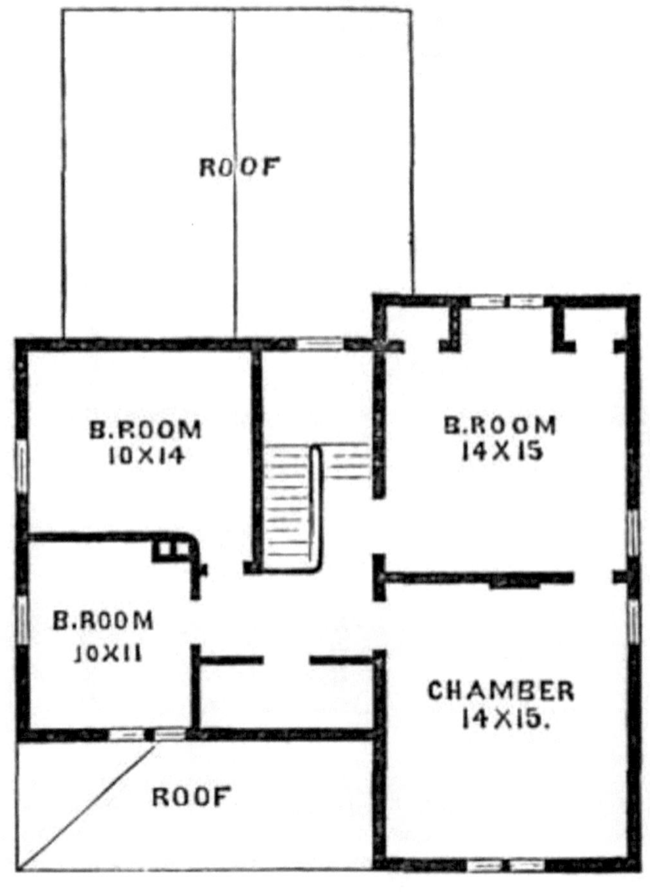

Fig. 44.—*Second Floor.*

This house is supplied with a cistern, constructed with the utmost care, ten feet in diameter, and ten [73] feet deep, holding 6,000 gallons of water. The roof is of slate, and the rain-water is therefore of great purity, free from color, and the woody taste usually imparted to it by falling on a shingle roof.

At the laundry sink is one of West's lift and force pumps, which draws the water from the cistern. This pump is a simple and effective affair, and works with remarkable ease, is always in order, and may be considered one of the best pumps known. We have given it a thorough trial, and speak from personal knowledge.

On one side of the laundry sink there is also one of Kedzie's large size rain-water filters, which holds several pails full of water, and which we commend as an admirable contrivance for the purposes intended. It possesses every merit claimed for it, and after more than a year's use, the water drawn from it is of such crystal purity and sweetness as to attract the attention of all to whom it is offered.

No well has been dug or contemplated on the premises connected with this cottage. About one-half the cost of a well has been expended upon a slate roof, a large and carefully-constructed cistern, West's pump and Kedzie's filter—the other half has been safely invested in U. S. 7-30's, and instead of hoisting water fifty feet, for household, garden, and stable uses, the turn of a croton water tap is not more easy and convenient, [74] and the finest flow of a silver spring of soft water, is not more beautiful than that delivered by West's pump and Kedzie's filter, which supplies for all purposes of the cottage, stable, and garden, water unsurpassed in its pleasant and wholesome properties. Those who seek the most convenient and reliable modes of procuring the purest and sweetest water, will find this to be the least costly and the most satisfactory.

For a compact, convenient cottage, with every facility for doing the work of the household, with the least number of steps—in which all the essential modern conveniences are introduced, without the modern prices attached—for a low-priced, elegant cottage, we do not know of any plan more appropriate than this.

In the construction of this house a bay-window was introduced in front, in the parlor, (Fig. 43.) and the veranda was made half octagon. These alterations add much to exterior appearance, as well as to the capacity of the parlor. On the side of the parlor and dining room an addition is contemplated, which will relieve the apparent want of variety which now exists, and essentially improve the external appearance.

[75]

DESIGN No. 14.

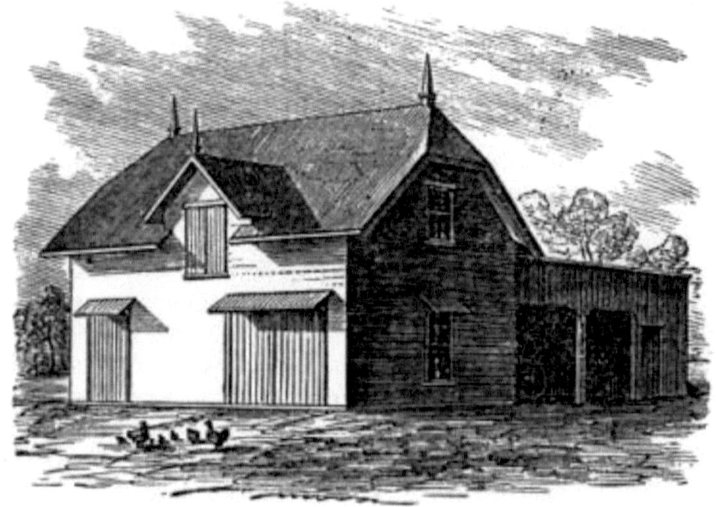

Fig. 45. — *Cottage Stable.*

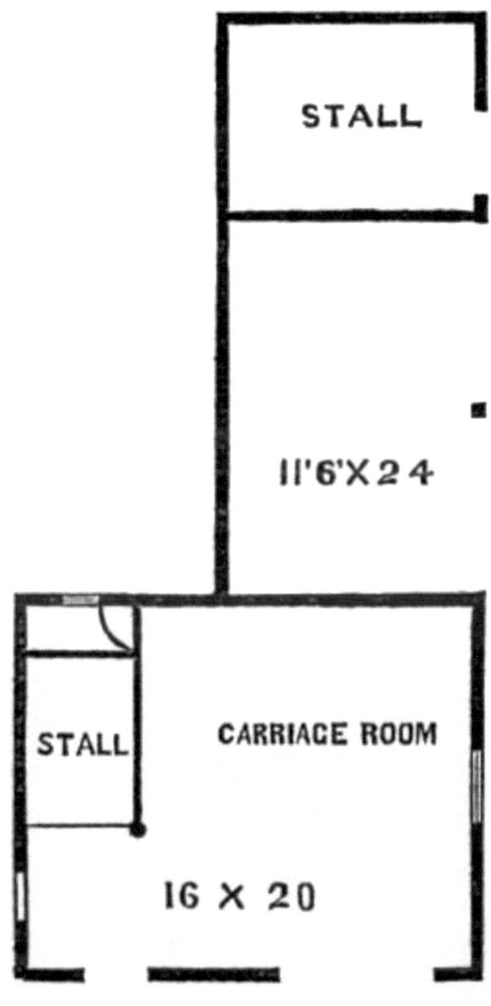

Fig. 46.—*Plan.*

[76]

Fig. 45 shows a design for a cottage stable, giving accommodations for a horse and cow, two carriages, one or two wagons, and two tons of hay. The main building is so proportioned, that three more stalls may be added, and it may then become the wing of a larger building, to be used for carriage room and other purposes.

For those who keep but one horse and cow, this design affords abundant room.

DESIGN No. 15.

ICE HOUSE.

It is only within a few years that ice, in all seasons, has been classed among the necessaries of life. In large cities it is indispensable, but the cool spring-house or cellar in the country impresses many with the idea that ice, in summer months, can only be regarded as a luxury. Along with other conveniences in keeping with this progressive age, the ice-house has its place, and a country-seat of any pretensions is not complete without it.

It is simple in construction, and can be built very cheaply of rough materials, or made as elaborate as is desirable. It forms a pretty feature about the grounds, if treated with some architectural taste. [77]

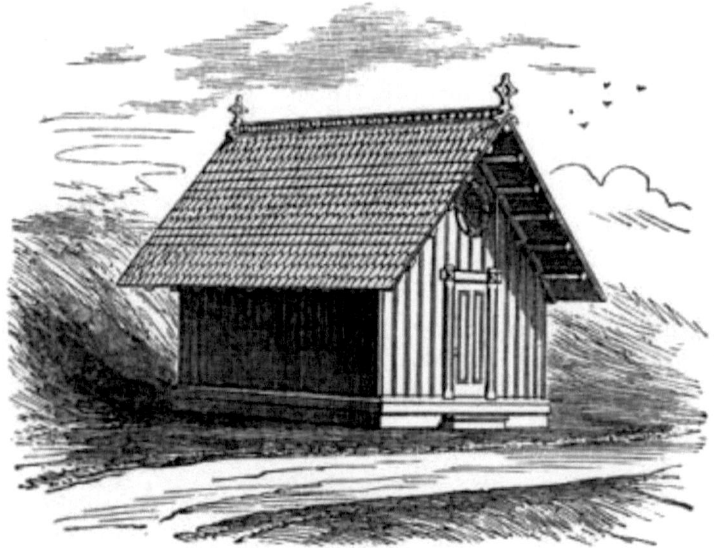

Fig. 47. — *Ice House.*

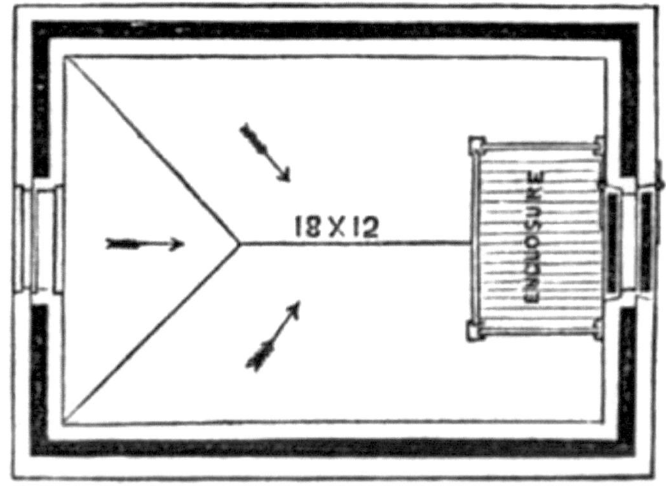

Fig. 48.—*Ground Plan.*

[78]

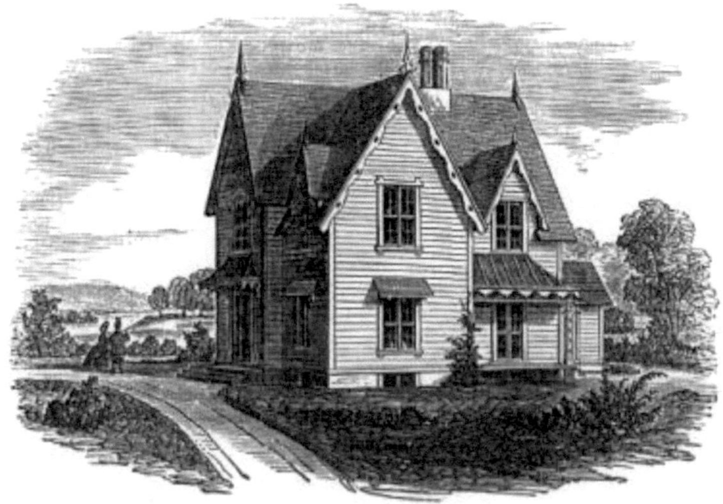

Fig. 49.—*Perspective.*

[79]

DESIGN No. 16.

This design, with the accompanying plans sufficiently explain themselves without minute description. The arrangement, as will be seen upon examination, secures a very large amount of accommodation, with good sized rooms, and ample store and closet conveniences. The building is compact, and at the same time presents a pleasing variety in its exterior appearance. By carrying up the library, two dressing rooms, for the two principal chambers, may be secured.

When one contemplates building, and has put his thoughts and wishes into a tangible form, the leading question asked is, how much will all this cost? for what price in dollars and cents, without extras or additional charges of any kind, can this dwelling be erected in a good and workmanlike manner, in accordance with plans and specifications, and satisfactory to the owner? This is precisely the plain English of what a business man wants to know; for we hold that it is right and proper, that every one should look right through all the connected links and complications that require a considerable expenditure of money, and see that he lands carefully in the place anticipated. To start with the intention of disbursing $5,000, and wind up with an expenditure of $12,000, is not only [80] annoying in a money point of view, but an impeachment of one's judgment and good sense, not pleasant to hear outsiders reflect on; for however much one might wish to shift the responsibility on others, it is one of those things that time will always place where it belongs. As long as men consider the arts of designing and constructing buildings to be of no special importance, or that they are qualified, without instruction or experience, to practice them, expensive blunders will naturally result, and sooner or later it will be discovered that such wisdom is dearly bought. There are many, however, who prefer to manage their building affairs thus, and who can only learn more agreeable and less expensive modes by actual experience; some do it from ignorance, some from supposed economy, and others from the supposition that they are best qualified.

The design for a house or other building, and a plan of the interior arrangement of each floor, prepared by a professional man who makes such things the business of his life, is now very generally admitted by intelligent men to be essential; but the management or superintendence of the work by the party who has studied and designed it, does not seem quite so apparent. An architect prepares the drawings for a dwelling to cost $5,000; now whether it actually will cost $5,000, $8,000 or $10,000, in the hands of another [81] superintendent, is an unanswered problem. A prevailing folly which we find very general, is to suppose that all men can build the same house, in all places, for precisely the same amount of money; and but few are willing to admit that they, of all others, are not the most competent to carry through the whole business of building at the lowest figure. Some must find out in the most expensive manner, that the profession of an architect, or the skill of a builder, can only be attained by long years of careful application.

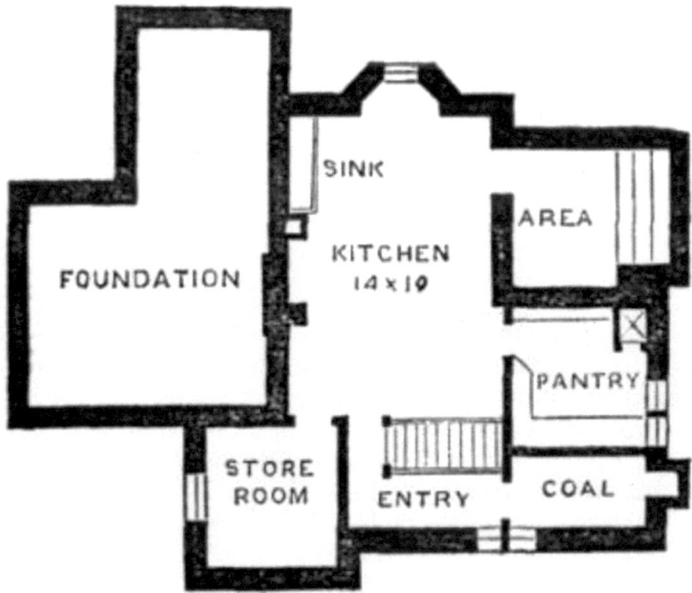

Fig. 50.—*Basement Plan.*

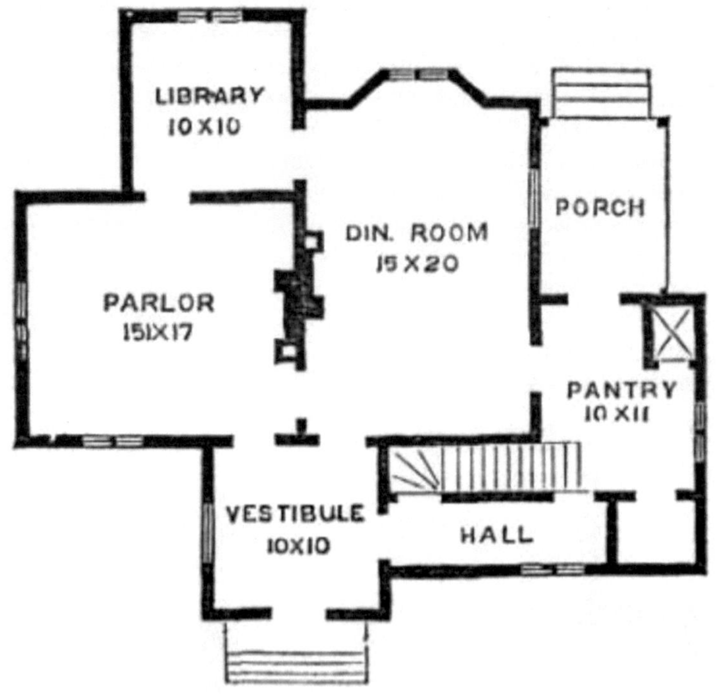

Fig. 51.—*First Floor.*

What a house will cost to build is a question always asked with the utmost simplicity, and a prompt and reliable answer always expected, and if not forthcoming at once, gives rise to a suspicion that one's professional ability is not of the most thorough character. [82] There are so many conditions to govern results in house building, that even an approximate estimate may fall very wide of the mark. Two houses may be built from the same plan, and we may also say, from the same specifications; one by day's work, and the other by contract, and they shall be so exactly alike in all respects when finished, that an unprofessional observer would detect no difference, and yet one may honestly cost just double the amount in money expended on the other; even the same builder may build two houses precisely alike in all respects, and yet the cost be quite unequal. On one site stone may be easily obtained, a sand bank on the premises, a running brook close at hand, saw mills, brick yards,

70

and [83] lime kilns within moderate distances and accessible by good roads. The other site may be quite the reverse in situation, or have some decided disadvantages in obtaining some very necessary materials. We once built a fine stone house where stone was abundant and close at hand, but all the lumber and brick had to be hauled thirteen miles over hilly roads; the cost of that house has nothing to do with the cost of a similar house in a different locality.

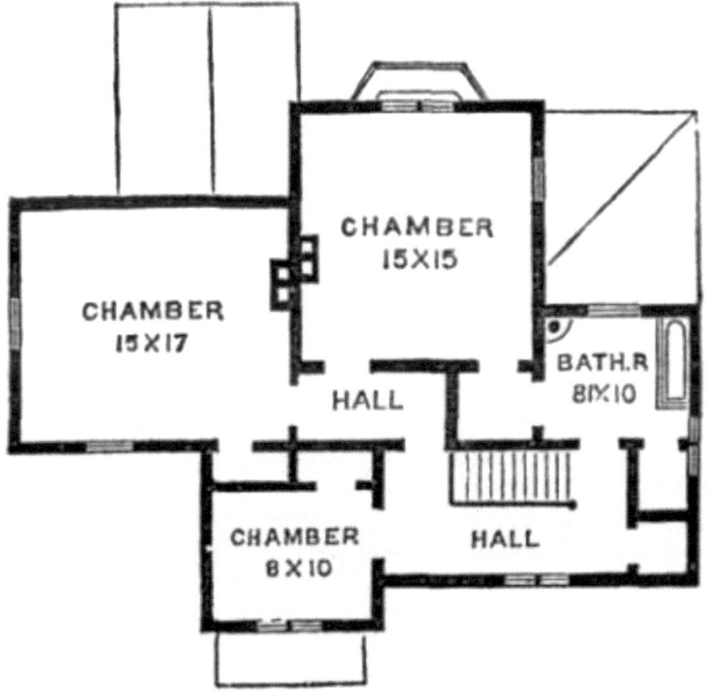

Fig. 52. — *Second Floor.*

A competent business superintendent has a great deal to do with the cost of a house; one that understands all the tricks of every building trade, that knows the market well, and the value and quality of all building materials, and where inferior workmanship [84] and materials can be used to an equal advantage with those of first class. To slight work and yet do it justice; to give it all the strength and endurance necessary, requires one of skillful acquirements. A mechanic may persuade a proprietor into many a long day's work, as it pays well to nurse good jobs when other work is slack, but an architect who understands such things would save the value of useless work.

The cost of a house depends on a well-studied plan; this plan does not consist alone in the arrangement of rooms, windows, doors, etc., but involves a careful study of the anatomy of construction. One may save by a proper distribution of timbers, as well as make a very great saving by the arrangement of rooms. Good management is of the greatest importance, not only as a matter of economy, but as securing the best class of workmanship, and the most judicious use of materials. Good or bad management produces the same results in building operations as in war or any other pursuit.

One takes up a capital work on rural architecture, written perhaps ten or fifteen years ago, before the general introduction of furnaces, steam pipes, gas, baths, marble basins, etc.; they find a house that suits them, which the book says will cost $6,000, and that is just the amount, by close figuring, that can be raised for building. The house is ordered, put in the [85] hands of the best mechanic to finish all complete, and he goes ahead; he is unrestricted except by the book, and the author of it is a man of reputation. In the way of details perhaps nothing has been said; they are therefore extravagant in the use of materials, and elaborate in workmanship; as it is not considered good policy for a workman who has a good order, to make suggestions calculated to decrease the amount of work. When the bills to the amount of $6,000 have been settled, the house is found to be half finished, and an additional $6,000 is necessary to complete it; less that one year's interest of which would have amply sufficed to secure the services of one who has spent the best years of his life to learn how to design and to manage work to cost a specified price.

When an architect says a house can be built for a certain price, it is to be understood that materials delivered on the ground shall not exceed an average cost, that the payments made are to be in cash, and that he manages the work. To hold an architect responsible or blame him for blunders in the cost of work that he designed and did not superintend, is manifestly unjust, yet it is a frequent occurrence.

The cost of work is a question easily answered, when one is fully acquainted with all its bearings and has it under his control, but no one can say at what price a novice in building operations can execute it.

[86]

DESIGN No. 17.

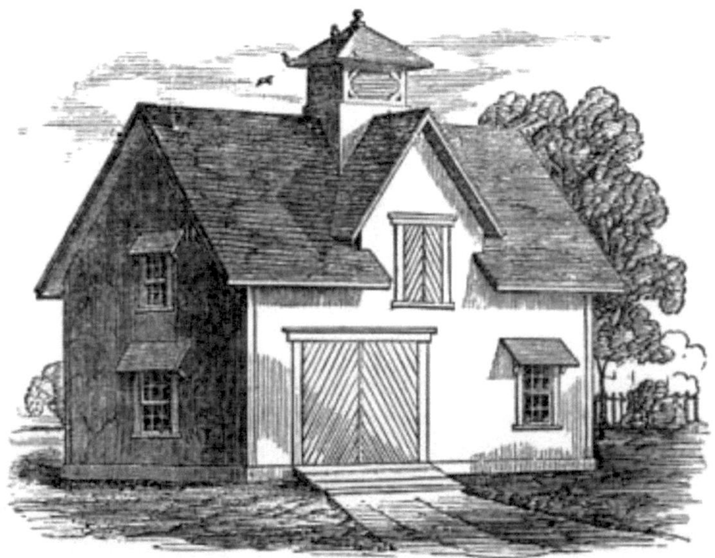

Fig. 53. — *Stable.*

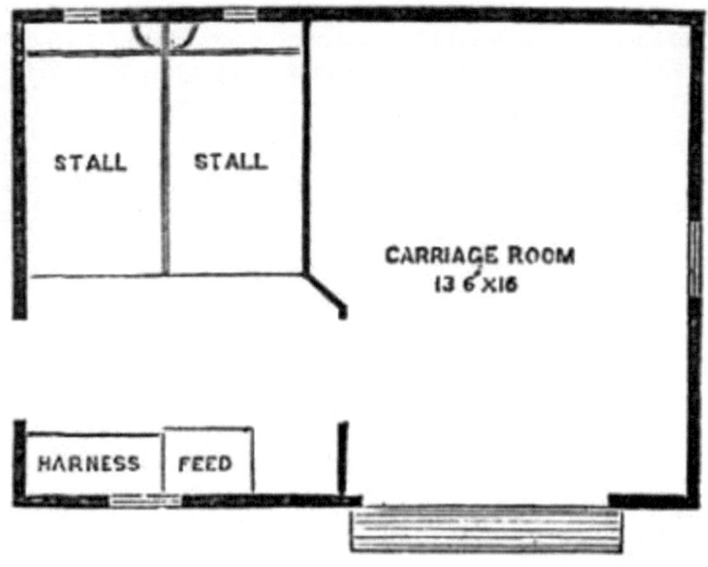

Fig. 54.— *Stable Plan. (Reversed.)*

Fig. 53 is a design for a cottage stable, with stalls for two horses, and the necessary carriage room and other conveniences. This design, in its exterior, presents [87] as great a degree of variety in the combinations of form and shadow as the price will admit of. It answers the purposes of comfortable protection and convenience, as well or even better than the most costly structures. A horse needs a dry, well-ventilated apartment, and enjoys fresh air, daylight, and sunlight as well as human beings. Unless these very inexpensive wants are provided, no compensation is afforded by elaborate detail and workmanship.

DESIGN No. 18.

SCHOOL HOUSE AT IRVINGTON, ON THE HUDSON.

Our architectural series would be by no means complete if devoted entirely to dwellings; and as the resources of an extensive professional practice in the arts which embellish and beautify our country may be largely made use of, we present here a design for another class of buildings.

A school-house is not a building which every one contemplates erecting, and yet a large proportion are, or ought to be, interested in developing in structures of this class such architectural principles as shall make their impressions in early life, and influence future tastes. [88]

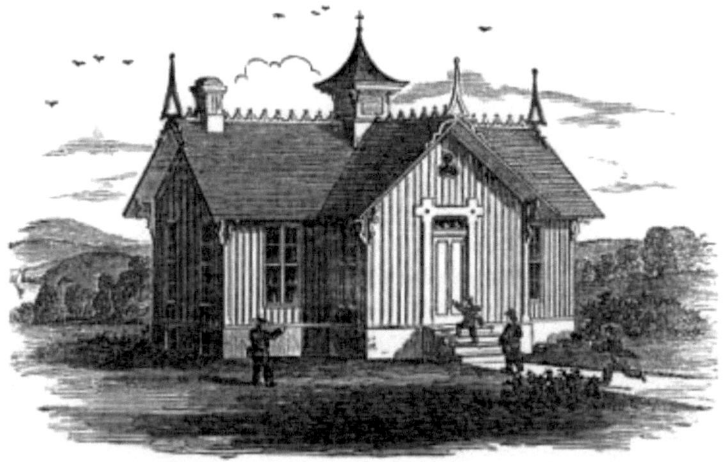

Fig. 55.—*School House.*

[89]

This building is designed to accommodate about fifty scholars, being 25 by 40 feet, with a front projection 10 by 18 feet. In the basement a large furnace and abundant accommodation for coal. The main floor is divided into school-room, two recitation rooms, hat and coat room, wash closet with sink, and water closet, above which is a large tank, supplied from the roof. An outside cistern supplies cool drinking-water, the purest and healthiest water known, and renders the use of ice unnecessary in summer. The height of all these ceilings is nearly fourteen feet, and each room is thoroughly ventilated; the belfry is provided with a one hundred pound bell; indeed, nothing has been left undone that is calculated to promote the health and comfort of the pupils.

The partition between the doors to the recitation rooms is made in sections, and can be easily removed, thus making one large room for exhibition and lecture purposes. The stage, in this case is to be placed at the left end of the room. The capacity of the building can be nearly doubled by occupying the entire floor as a school-room, and building an addition 12 by 24 feet directly in the rear, opposite to the front projection, for recitation rooms.

The situation of this building at Irvington, on the Hudson, some twenty-five miles above the city of New York, is in a charming, healthy, and delightful [90] locality; one made famous by the pen and residence of Washington Irving, and noted for its magnificent scenery, its views of river and mountain, and the fine taste displayed in landscape and architectural embellishments by those who have made their homes in this vicinity.

We have always thought that those educational institutions possess the most attractions that are so situated that all surroundings shall have a favorable influence; and there is nothing like example in early training. Bring up and educate a boy among those who know nothing of the refinements of life, away from the progressive examples of art and taste, in a tumble-down, unplastered, ill-heated and ventilated apartment, and he never can become, with all the aid of books and teachers, as thoroughly cultivated and fitted for the duties of life, as one who has enjoyed associations of a higher order. School architecture has a meaning in it; there is value in proportion, harmony, beauty, light and shade, as applied to school buildings, that is not comprehended by all. A recent writer says better than we can say it, that "It is the duty of teachers, as well as parents and school committees, to see that the circumstances under which children study are such as shall leave a happy impression upon their minds; for whatever is brought under the frequent observation of the young must have its [91] influence upon their susceptible natures for good or evil. Shabby school-houses induce slovenly habits. Ill-constructed benches may not only distort the body, but, by reflex influence, the mind as well. Conditions like these seldom fail to disgust the learner with his school, and neutralize the best efforts of his teachers. On the other hand, neat, comfortable places for study may help to awaken the associations enchaining the mind and the heart to learning and virtuous instruction with links of gold brightening forever."

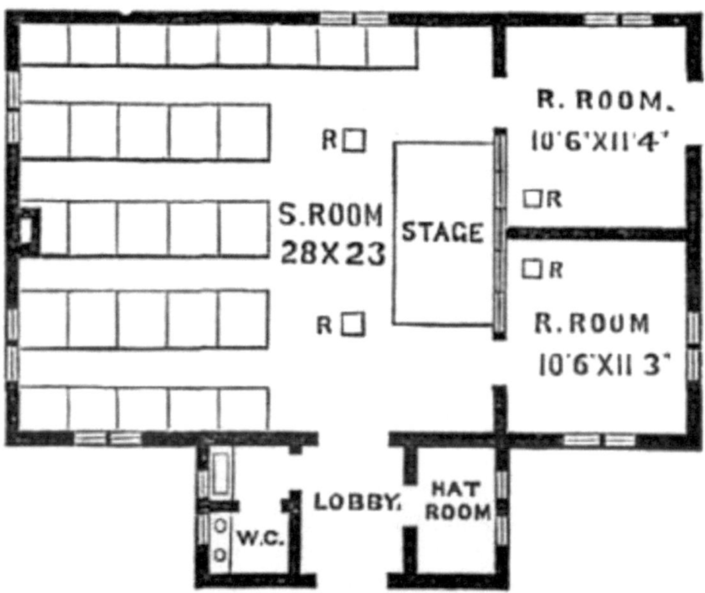

Fig. 56.—*Principal Floor.*

[92]

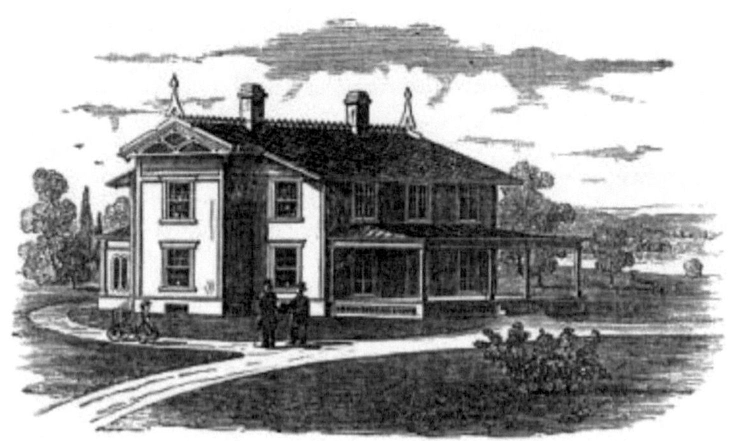

Fig. 57.—*Perspective View.*

[93]

DESIGN No. 19.

This design was prepared for erection in the vicinity of Goshen, Orange Co., N. Y., and the accommodation limited to a price not exceeding − −. It presents in hall, verandas, and large parlor, some of the very necessary attractions of a country house, and is a good example of what can be done for a limited sum. While the plan is a parallelogram, and the roof free from hips and valleys, the general arrangement is such as to show considerable variety in outline, and one, we think, that will have a pleasing effect.

Such houses, erected in the vicinity of New York, and many of our large cities, would add a large value to the ground they stand on, and pay a handsome rate of interest on their cost; better than any other class of building investments, as the supply is in nowise equal to the demand. It is so simple a matter, with present prompt and rapid railroad facilities, to invite a fair proportion of the young business men of our large cities to make their homes in the adjoining country, that we wonder capitalists and real estate owners do not more frequently make money for themselves and others by erecting tasteful, low-priced suburban homes. [94]

78

In former times, a house of this class erected in the country, would be painted exteriorly a pure white, with no relief, except probably in the violent contrast of bright green venetian blinds to the windows. This sort of taste unfortunately still remains, although in the progress of rural taste and art, the country is much improved in this respect.

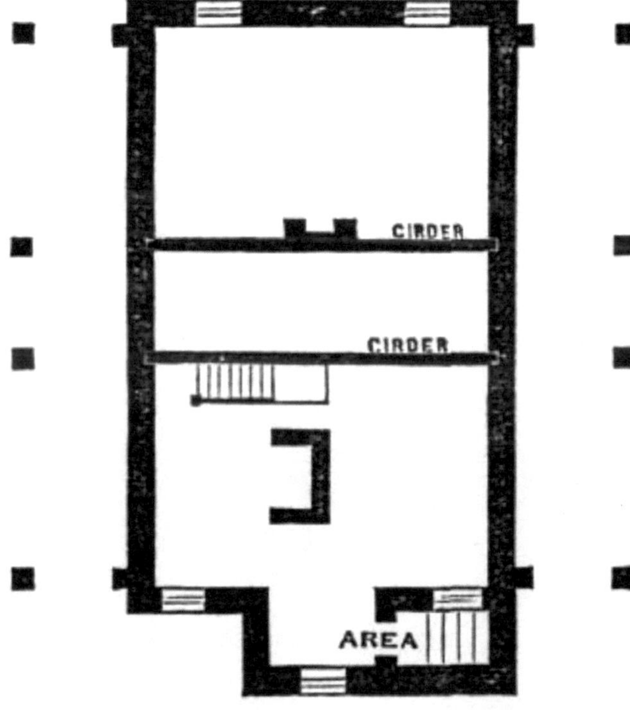

Fig. 58. — *Cellar.*

There is a variety of colors, known as neutral tints, which are suitable for exteriors, and the effect produced by them is altogether pleasing, while a house painted white can never be an agreeable object in any landscape, however admirable its architectural proportions and finish may be. [95]

The tone of color for a house will depend upon its size, form, and situation, and it often requires a nice and cultivated eye to determine what would be most appropriate and effective.

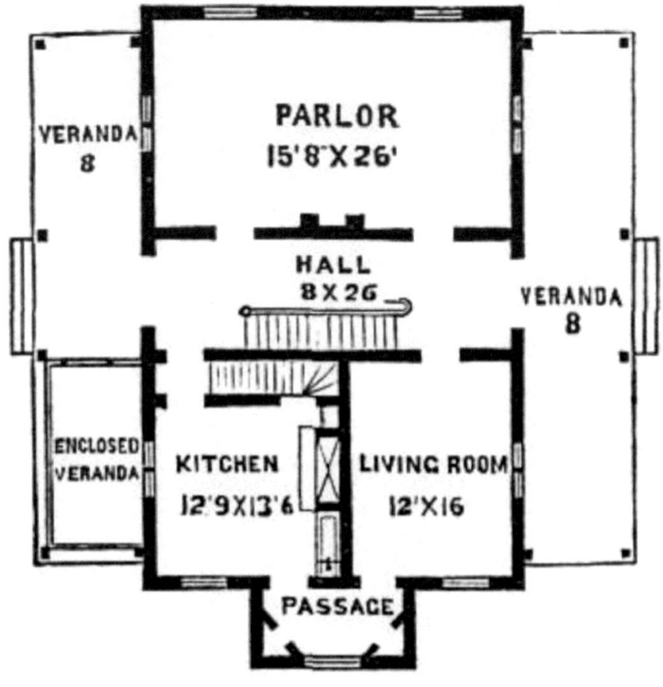

Fig. 59.—*First Floor.*

For such a house as this, we should choose a light fawn color—not yellow—and paint the cornice, window-frames and other projecting and ornamental parts two or three shades darker than the body of the building. This will give a depth of shadow and expression which cannot be obtained in any other way.

Large houses, with massive features of construction, will bear to be painted with darker colors, but they should not be too sombre, so as to give a gloomy appearance to the house. The country, with its bright [96] sunshine, its rich adornments of flowers, and its numberless forms of beauty and grace, is eminently cheerful. It often happens that the painter does all he can to mar this cheerfulness and beauty, by startling contrasts of colors, and by destroying the harmony which pervades the landscape.

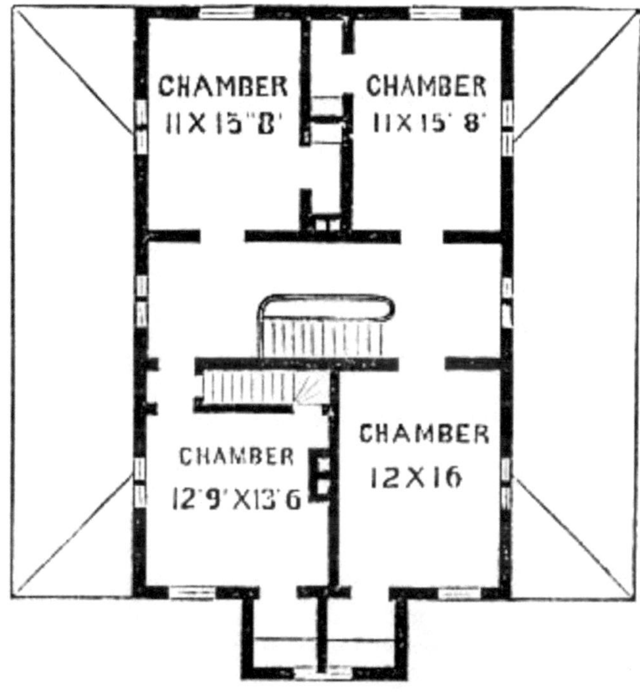

Fig. 60. — *Second Floor*.

DESIGN No. 20.

A COUNTRY CHAPEL.

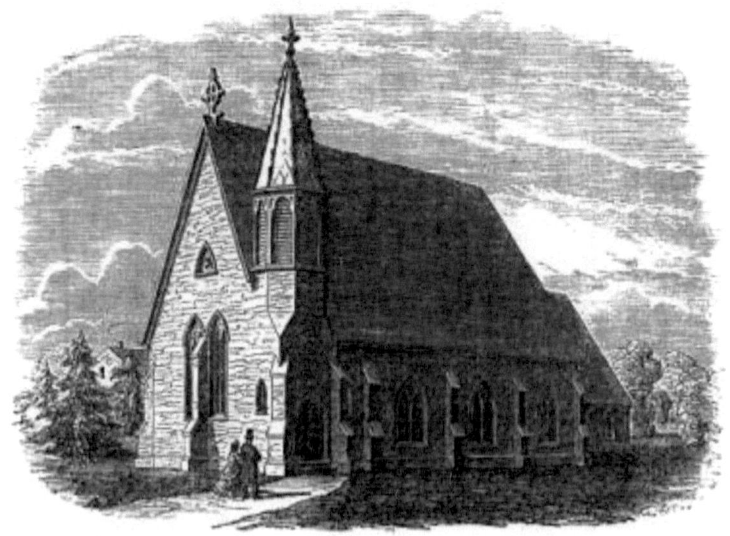

Fig. 61. — *Perspective.*

We present in this design a plan for a substantial and permanent chapel, having capacity for seating about four hundred. For the purpose for which it [98] [97] was designed, no distinct chancel was required. Such a chancel could be arranged, if desired, in a recess taken off the lecture or class room in the rear of the chapel. It could be lighted at the roof, or on the sides.

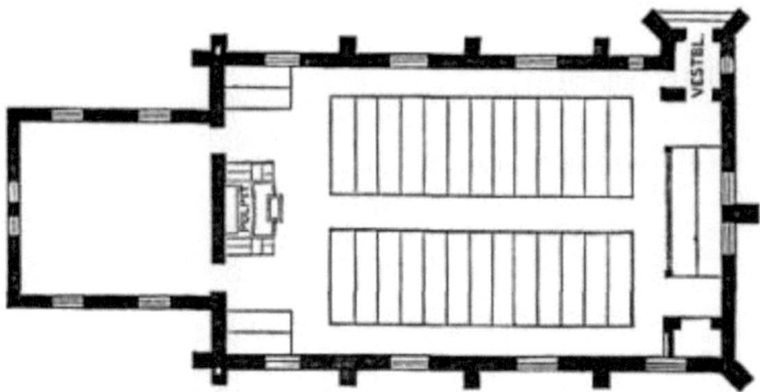

Fig. 62. — *Ground Plan.*

82

This chapel, built of stone throughout, with an open timber roof and stained glass windows, would be an ornament to any country locality, and a credit to the taste and liberality of those who built it.

Every thing about such a chapel should be *real*, and no suspicion of sham or unreality should be tolerated in any part of the work. The practice of building the fronts of churches of stone, while the side and rear walls are constructed of rough brick, painted and marked off to resemble the stone, is very common, we [99] know, both in town and country, but it is a species of deceit and false pretence which ought not to be. If the best and costliest material cannot be used for the entire structure, let the rougher and inferior material be fairly shown, in every part. If the means and liberality of the parish cannot provide oak or walnut for the interior finish, let the wood work be plainly painted, or what is better still, simply oiled, but there should be no cunning deception of graining, to represent the costlier wood. It is not *honest*, and, we take it, a church, built for religious worship, is the last place that should betray our human meanness and want of honesty.

DESIGN No. 21.

We show in this design what can be done with a substantial old farm house; how easily and beautifully it can be changed into a suburban home of elegant exterior, and comfortable and convenient interior appointments.

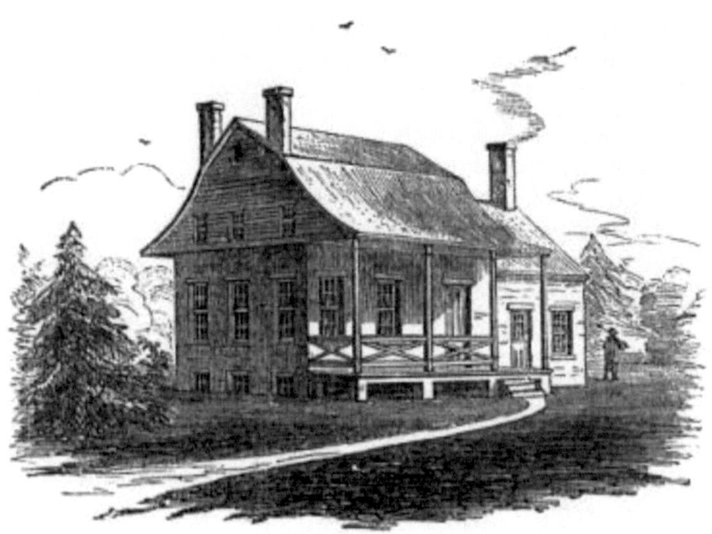

Fig. 63. — *View of the House at the time of Purchase.*

This class of spacious and substantial farm houses, with the gambrel, curb, or Mansard roof, as shown in Fig. 63, is very numerous about the suburbs of New [102] [101] [100] York City, and more particularly in the "neighboring province of New Jersey," where one finds them nestled in the valleys or by the road side, as best fitting to the taste of our early Dutch settlers, who prized seclusion and protection above bleak exposure and far-reaching views.

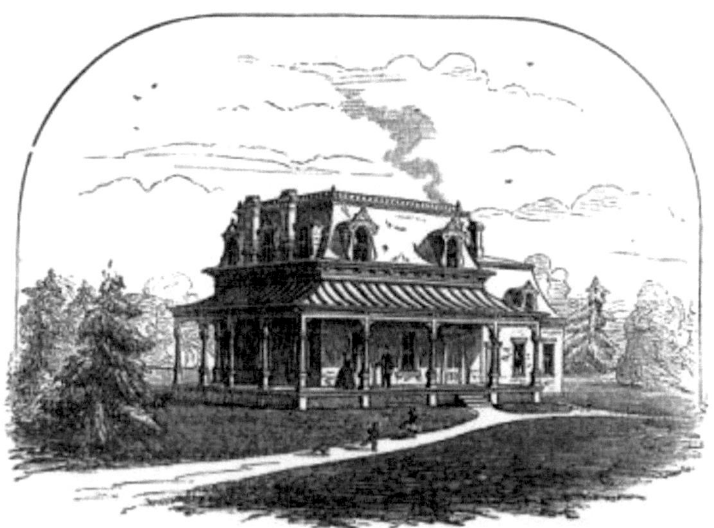

Fig. 64.—*The same remodeled.*

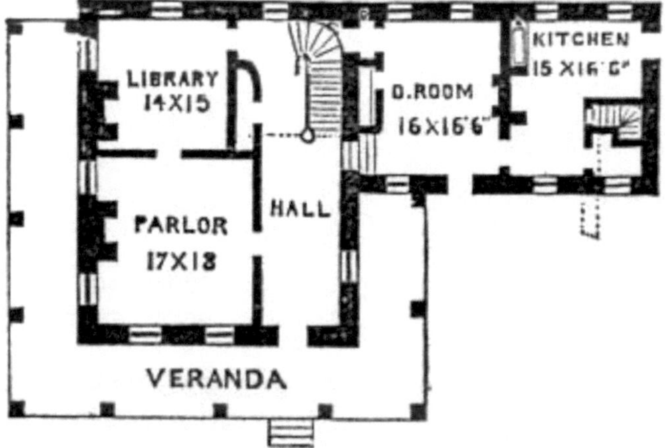

Fig. 65.

As a general thing, the better class of New Jersey farm houses of this type were built of squared and hammered red sand-stone, laid up in regular courses, and in many instances the character of the work differed on all sides, the front being the most finely finished.

And in many of the most pretentious of these houses, brick was substituted for the front, as being less common.

There is, perhaps, nothing more difficult in an architect's experience than to make a fine thing out of a subject so destitute of beauty of form or proportion, [103] and yet preserve the substantial walls and other belongings, that have stood for half a century, and are now stronger, and promise a durability that exceeds those of other houses built in this progressive age; and yet here is a "presto change" that will almost defy the keen eyes of the old settlers to recognize any trace of the ancient landmark that for fifty years has overlooked the beautiful valley of the Tenakill.

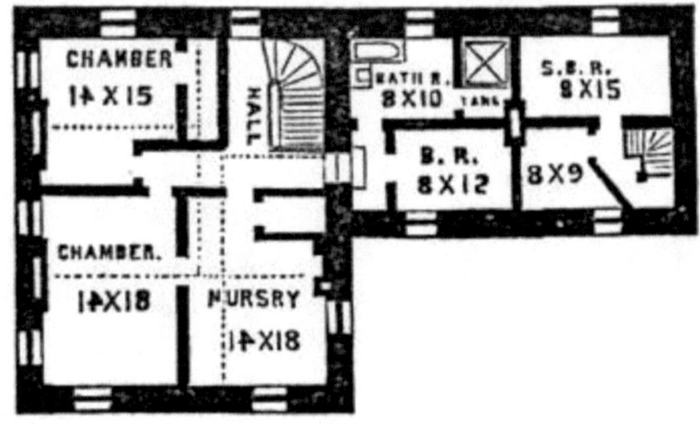

Fig. 66.

There are very many of these old houses that are equally well adapted to wear a modern face, though but few purchasers can look through all such changes with the eye of a professional expert, and select that to which, at a low price, a certain beauty can be added, which, when done, shall indicate the wisdom of their choice. First impressions many times are sadly against all hopes of success.

> "With weather-stains upon the wall,
> And stairways worn, and crazy doors,
> And creaking and uneven floors,
> And chimneys huge, and tiled and tall."

But these difficulties are the least troublesome to [104] adjust, if the walls are good, and ceilings of a fair modern height. It may then be a better choice to adapt such a house to the present cultivated tastes and requirements, than to build anew from the foundation.

In the plans, the dotted lines show the centers of the old partitions. Six feet have been added to the length of the wing, thus improving the kitchen accommodations.

This house is situated some fifteen miles from the great commercial metropolis, on one of the new lines of Railroad, and in a locality of easy access to New York business men.

DESIGN No. 22.

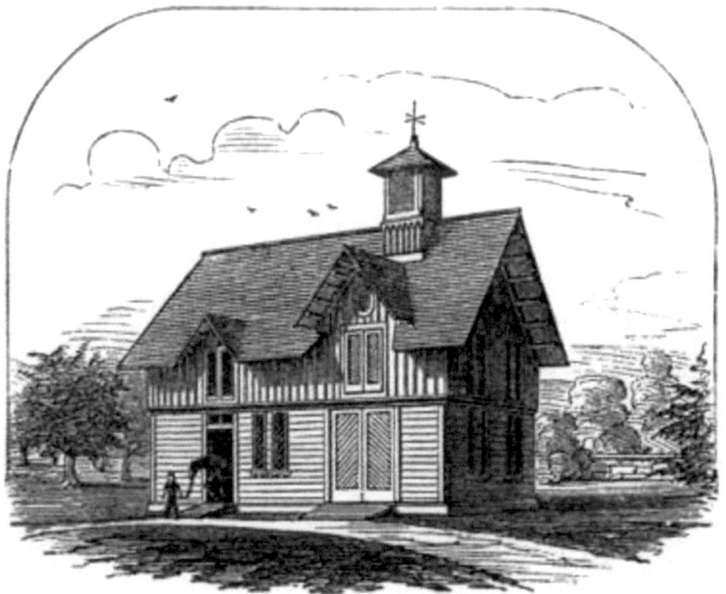

Fig. 67.—*Stable.*

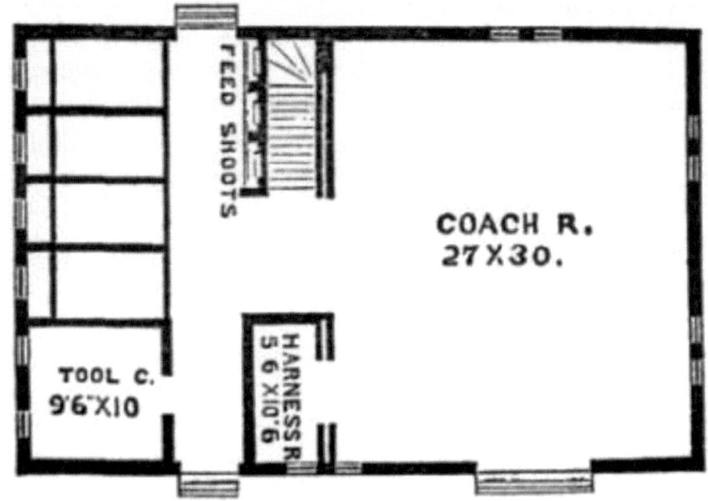

Fig. 68. — *Plan.*

This stable may be constructed either of wood, or of stone. It contains stalls for four horses, and affords space for their accommodation, together with a harness room and a tool closet. This latter is a convenience very essential to the comfort of the owner, as well as to the proper care and preservation of such implements [106] [105] as belong especially to the carriage house and stable.

This building should be surrounded and screened with fruit trees and shrubbery, and then, with its evident architectural effects, it will become an attractive feature in the landscape of which it becomes a part, with the other accessories of the elegant country home.

DESIGN No. 23.

FENCES.

In spite of all laws to the contrary, cattle will intrude upon one's property, and each and all must at great expense build and maintain fences for their own protection. There has not as yet been devised any practicable mode by which the enormous sums annually spent in fencing might be saved. The theory advanced, that it is cheaper for each to fence his cattle in, than to fence his neighbor's out, has not as yet been practically illustrated, if we except a few suburban localities. [107]

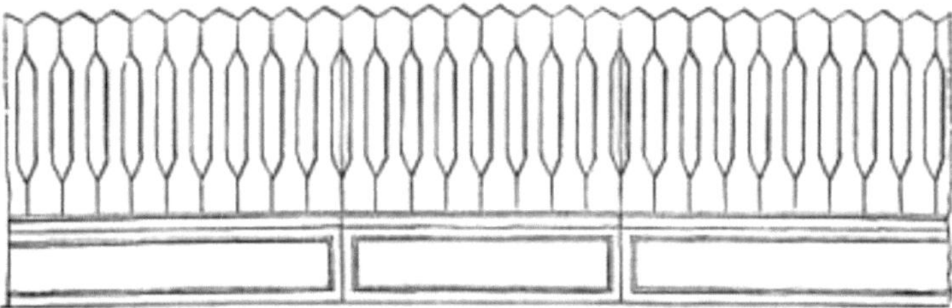

Fig. 69.

Fig. 69 represents a substantial fence, with a paneled base, of simple construction, and yet quite effective [108] in appearance. In Fig. 70 the work is somewhat more elaborate, while the base is of stone, or brick. Each engraving shows two panels, with a gate in the centre.

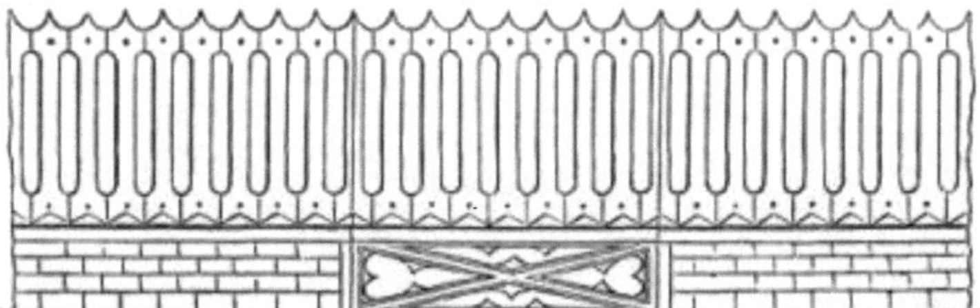

Fig. 70.

With chestnut or cedar posts, the pickets cut from 1½ inch plank, and the whole kept painted, such a fence would last many years.

DESIGN No. 24.

RESIDENCE OF CHARLES F. PARK, ESQ.

This residence of which we show only the floor plans, occupies a commanding position on the northern end of the Palisades, on the western side of the Hudson, some twenty miles above the city of New York, the river, mountain, and inland views from which are exceedingly fine, embracing the villages of Dobbs' Ferry, Irvington, Tarrytown, Sing Sing, Piermont, Nyack, and Tappan, as well as Tappan Zee and Haverstraw Bay, the distant Highlands of the Hudson, and the beautiful valleys of the Sparkill and the Hackensack, a section of country rich in historic associations, and highly appreciated by those who seek suburban homes. [109]

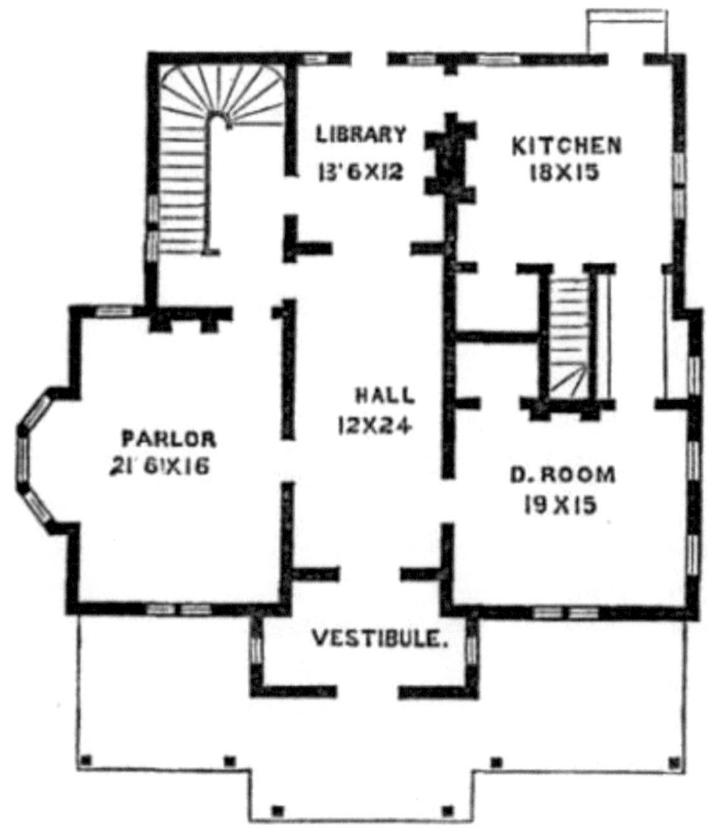

Fig. 71.—*First Floor.*

90

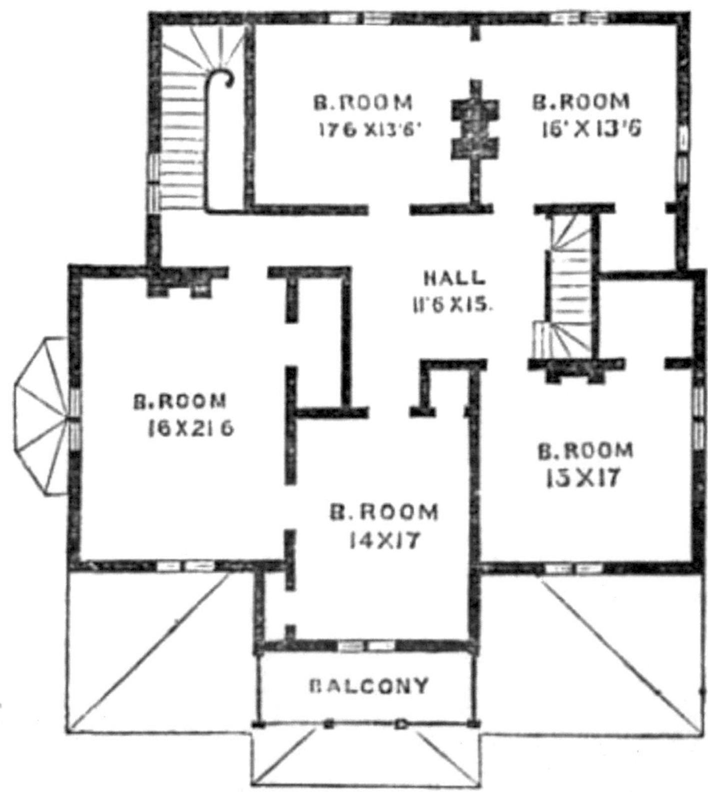

Fig. 72. — *Second Floor.*

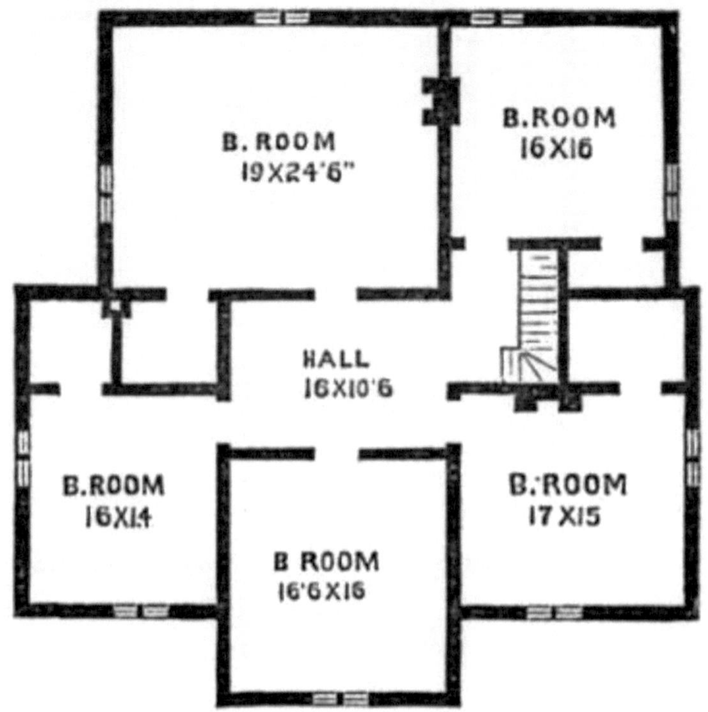

Fig. 73. — *Third Floor.*

This house was designed principally for a summer residence, being nearly fifty feet square, with wide halls and spacious verandah, and commodious and well ventilated sleeping apartments, the plans showing the arrangement of rooms. The style of architecture selected is that generally known as the Rural Gothic, which, perhaps, is the most useful and most beautiful of any that are adapted to the requirements of our climate. The almost square form of the plan is one of the most difficult to treat successfully in this style, yet has been carried out in the most satisfactory manner. This style admits of an almost never-ending [111] [110] variety of form and proportion, and in effects of light and shadow at all hours of day is unequaled. Its comparative expense but little exceeds the hipped and Mansard roofs.

92

The building is constructed in the most thorough and workman-like manner, and is as well adapted for a winter residence as for summer. The frame is built in the balloon style, (the strongest known form of framing,) with deep studding filled in with brick, having double air chambers, is thoroughly finished throughout, is covered with a slate roof, and fulfills all the requirements of a substantial and commodious country residence.

DESIGN No. 25.

CARRIAGE HOUSE AND STABLE.

The accompanying design for a carriage house and stable affords about the same amount of accommodation as Design 22. The arrangement, however, is somewhat different, and the exterior quite unlike it. In this plan the portion appropriated to the stalls is more ample, and the means for ventilation abundant. [112]

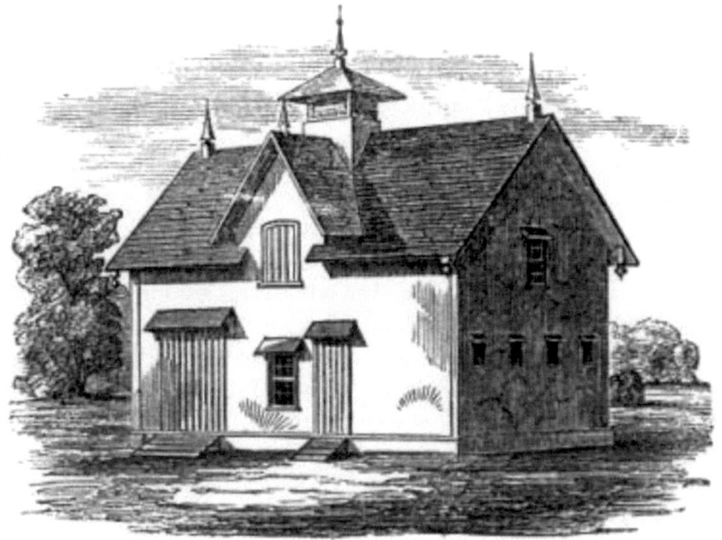

Fig. 74.—*Stable.*

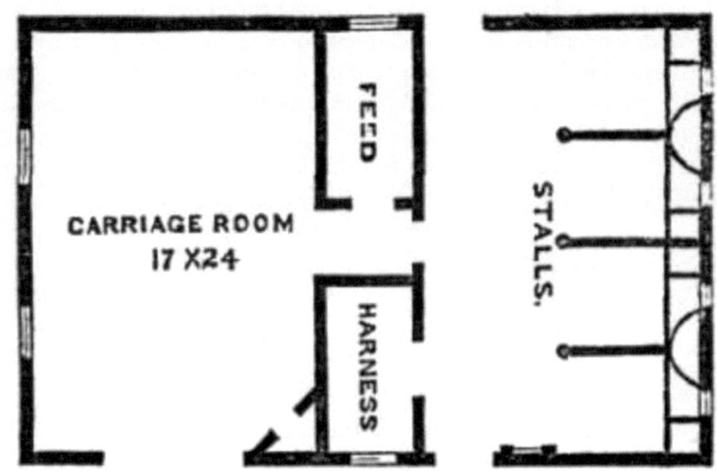

Fig. 75.—*Stable Plan.*

[113]

DESIGN No. 26.

RESIDENCE OF THOS. H. STOUT, ESQ.,

IRVINGTON, ON THE HUDSON.

Irvington is a noted locality for the higher grades of country homes, there being many fine examples of substantial, roomy, and elegantly appointed mansions. Far within the gradually extending circle which limits the daily intercourse of the business man to the city of New York, it has become, in virtue of its position, healthfulness, fine scenery, and ease of access, one of the most favored of the suburbs of this city; a city whose rapid increase of population and corresponding decreasing comforts in conveyance from one portion to another, is turning the attention of those who like ease of transit, and the quiet and health of the country, to a residence among its beautiful and attractive suburbs. What the last ten years have accomplished in introducing rapid and reliable communication, and building up and improving the country about New York, will prob-

94

ably be repeated several times over in the next decade. An impetus has been given to rural life, that will increase with every facility that is offered, and it will not be many years before the suburbs of New York will compare with any city in the world; and we question, even now, if elsewhere can be found a suburban locality [115] [114] comparable with the east bank of the Hudson, from New York to the Highlands.

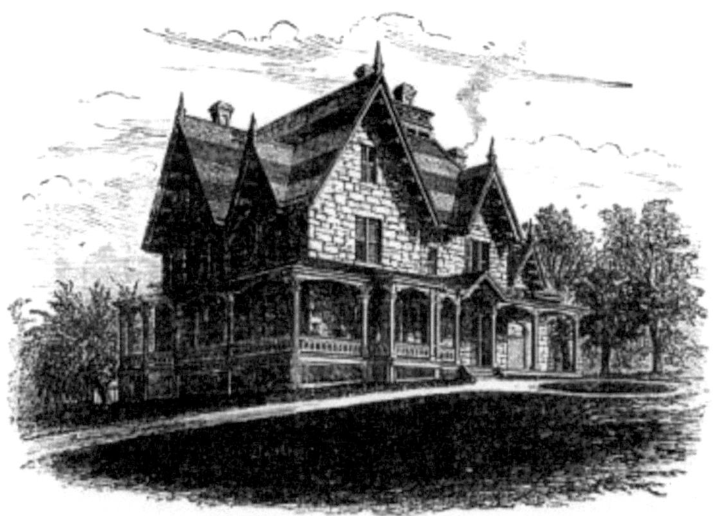

Fig. 76.—*Residence of Thos. H. Stout, Esq., Irvington, on the Hudson.*

The accompanying engravings illustrate a country house that embraces many of the best features of exterior variety, and interior compactness and convenience. The workmanship and materials throughout have been of the best description, and no pains have been spared to make it first class in every respect.

Situated on the slope of the eastern bank of the Hudson, it overlooks the broad expanse of "Tappan Zee," and commands the views peculiar to this locality, that reach from the Highlands to the ocean.

To build well, and to do so at a low price, is always desirable; and to build artistically, imposingly, attractively, does not imply elaborate finish or profuse ornament. Sand paper and decoration will never make an ill-proportioned building attractive to an educated taste, while a rough exterior of harmonious lines and forms will pass current with those who have an eye to the artistic.

One of the most important lessons that the art student learns is that of effect; that effects can not be produced by smoothly finished surfaces or details; and that in architecture, as well as in sculpture or painting, there must be a strong bold manner of execution, when there is a desire to convey an impression of strength or power. [116]

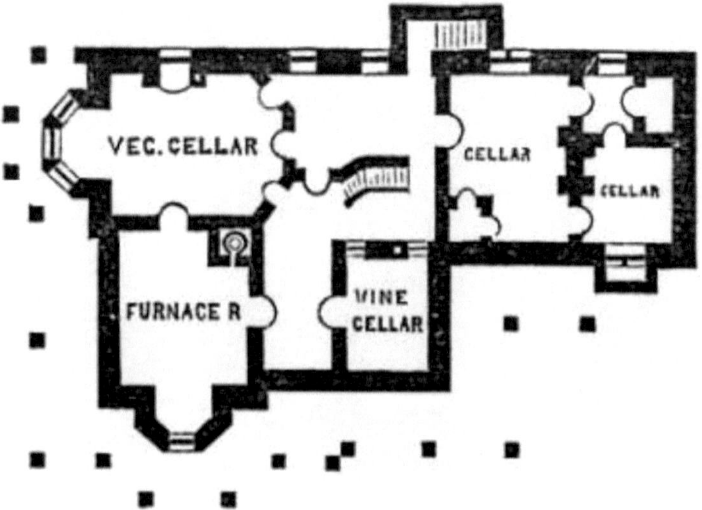

Fig. 77. — *Cellar.*

Where stone is conveniently obtained as a building material, its use in rural architecture deserves far more consideration than is usually bestowed on it; and in its unchiselled, quarried form it becomes desirable in an economical point of view. There is an imposing grandeur in the unhewn stone that asserts its presence in both near and distant views, and, with the proper combinations of proportion, and light and shade, will illustrate the finest architectural effects. Prevailing prejudices are too apt to consider it not only cheap, but inferior in protection and durability to finely wrought surfaces and smooth, close-fitting joints. We are too apt to estimate the value and beauty of a stone house by the amount of labor lavished on its exterior, as if the chisel possessed the power to make the joints more impenetrable, and [117] bestowed an endurance

96

commensurate with the story of expense that it tells. So long as we build well and honestly, with a proper regard to protection from the weather, in a substantial and workmanlike manner, good taste and sound sense will uphold the use of quarried rock, and discover a permanent strength and power in this Cyclopean masonry that elaborately finished surfaces and delicately wrought ornaments fail to express.

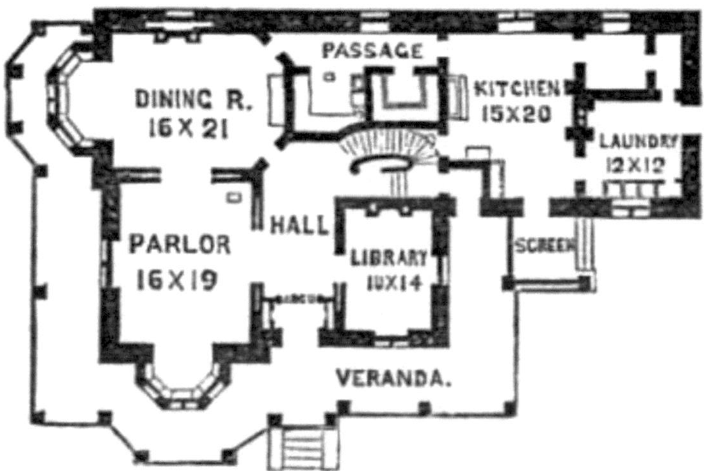

Fig. 78.—*First Floor.*

Dressed in squared blocks and hammered lines, stone becomes an expensive building material, and preference is then given to something else less costly; but if used in its quarried form, irregular in size and shape, it becomes, wherever conveniently obtained, among the economical materials used for building, and is unsurpassed for its impressiveness and durability. No paint is required to preserve it from the [118] weather, and no color is so good as the color of the stone; time softens its tints, and the clambering vine that lays hold of the massive walls is a decoration beyond the resources of architecture.

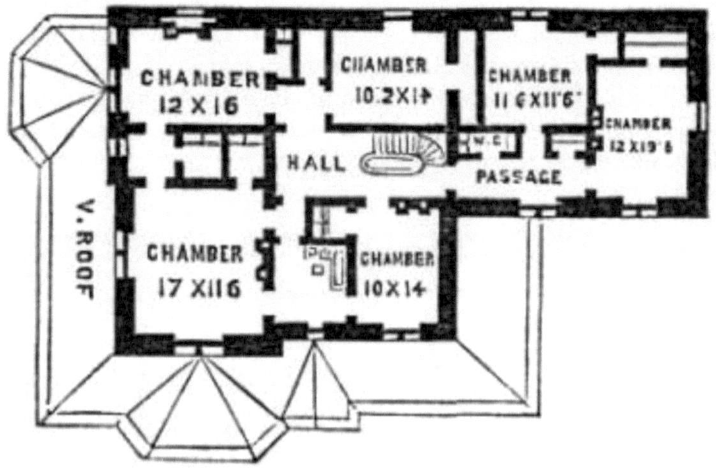

Fig. 79.—*Second Floor.*

"If a building," says Mr. Ruskin, "be under the mark of average magnitude, it is not in our power to increase its apparent size by any proportionate diminution in the scale of its masonry; but it may be often in our power to give it a certain nobility by building it of massy stones, or, at all events, introducing such into its make. Thus it is impossible that there should ever be majesty in a cottage built of brick; but there is a marked element of sublimity in the rude and irregular piling of the rocky walls of the mountain cottages of Wales, Cumberland, and Scotland.

"And if the nobility of this confessed and natural [119] masonry were more commonly felt, we should not lose the dignity of it by smoothing surfaces and fitting joints. The sums which we waste in chiselling and polishing stones, which would have been better left as they came from the quarry, would often raise a building a story higher.

"There is also a magnificence in the natural cleavage of the stone to which the art must indeed be great, that pretends to be equivalent; and a stern expression of brotherhood with the mountain heart from which it has been rent, ill-exchanged for a glistering obedience to the rule and measure of men. His eye must be delicate indeed who would desire to see the Pitti Palace polished."

98

DESIGN No. 27.

A CHAPTER ON GATES.

We present in the following designs, several illustrations of the principle of the truss applied to wooden gates. It was described by us, several years ago in the *Country Gentleman*.

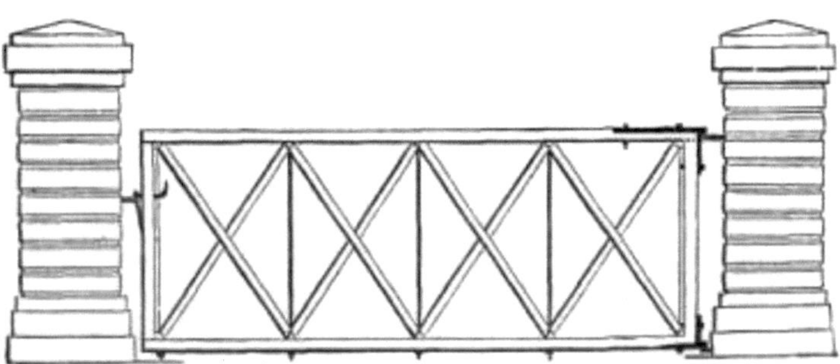

Fig. 80.

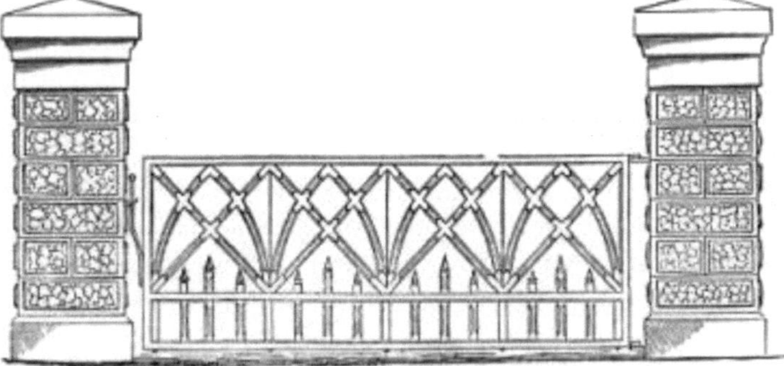

Fig. 81.

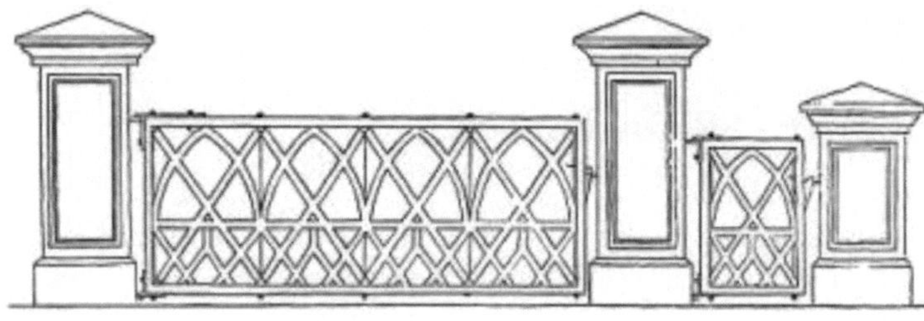

Fig. 82.

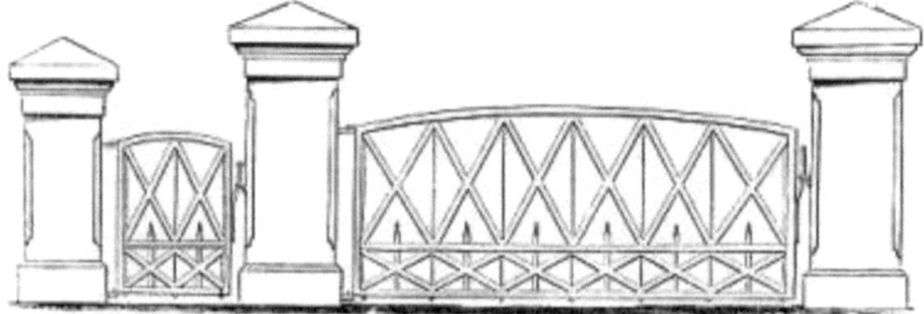

Fig. 83.

Since then, in our professional rambles, we have accidentally no-
ticed some thirty gates erected after [124] [123] [122] [121] [120]
these designs in different sections of the country, and, for aught we
know to the contrary, it is one of the most popular gates that swing.
The principle of this gate is best shown in figure 80, and consists of
four panels of braces crossing each other, and held firmly in position by five iron rods, which can be tightened by the screws at the
bottom. The braces are not tenoned, and there are no nails about the
gate. There can be no sagging under any circumstances; but should
such a thing occur from unequal shrinkage, it can easily be reme-
died by placing a thin strip of wood [125] or sheet lead under the
foot of the braces running forward. There is economy in the construction of these gates, as they can be made with a less number of
joints, and greater strength and stiffness secured with lighter materials, than in any other style of gate we know of. The principle is the
one used in railroad bridges and roofs of great span, and our own
experience with them, having built and tested all the gates [126]
here illustrated, is, that they possess very decided merits.

Fig. 81 is the principal entrance gate to one of the finest estates on the Hudson, above Tarrytown, and although similar in appearance to figure 82, has some very decided differences, the cross braces in this case reaching only to a second rail; the rods, however, pass through to the bottom; it is much more elaborate in workmanship, and the addition of a moulding on the top and bottom would increase its effect.

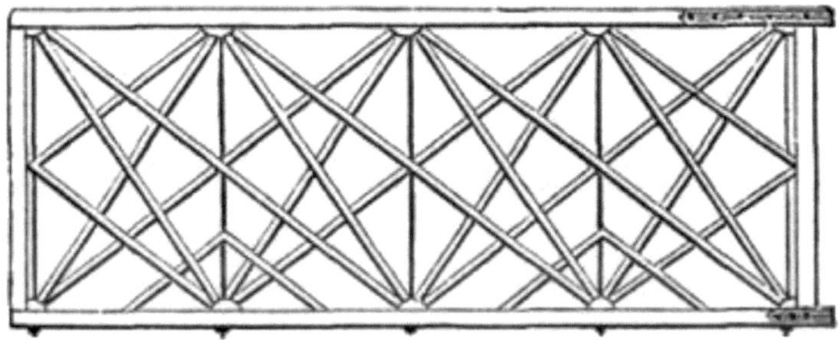

Fig. 84.

Fig. 84 is the entrance gate at the New Windsor, N. Y., Parsonage, and has been hanging six years without a perceptible change. The braces in this are one inch square and doubled; they are not halved, but cross each other, two one way and one the other, in the manner shown in figure 85. [127]

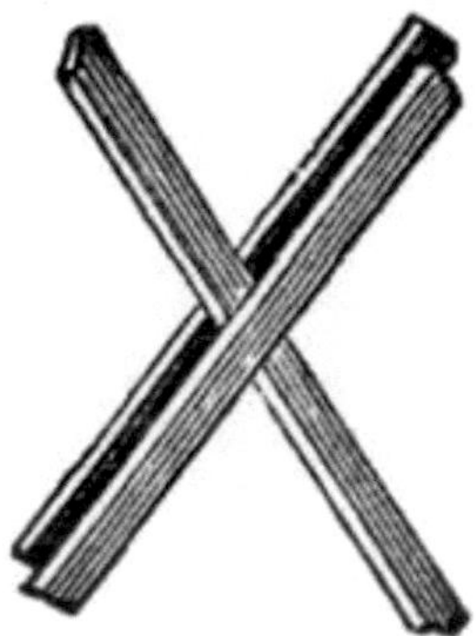

Fig. 85.

There is no other mode of constructing gates in which rustic work can be made such good use of. The chief objection to all things made in the rustic manner is, that they soon fall to pieces, limbs shrink and twist, and nails do not hold; but a rustic gate held together by iron rods will remain good until the last brace has decayed.

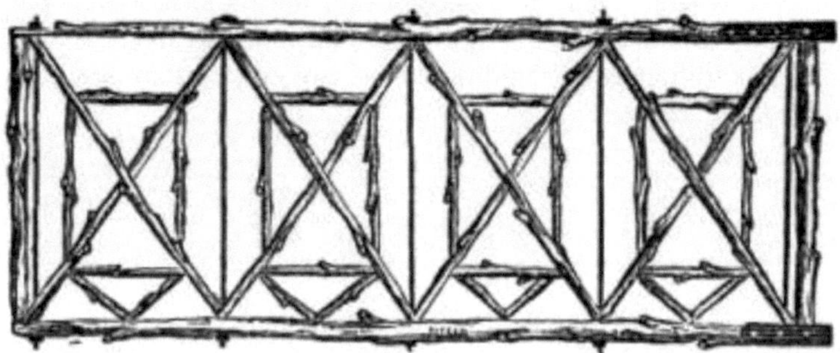

Fig. 86.

Fig. 86 is the principal entrance gate to one of the most finely finished country seats on Newburgh Bay.

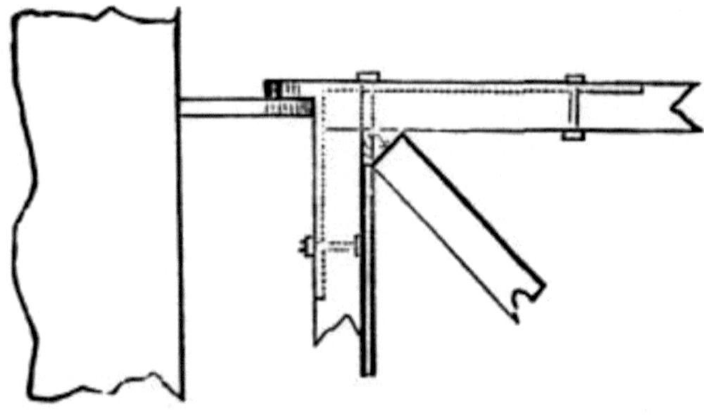

Fig. 87.

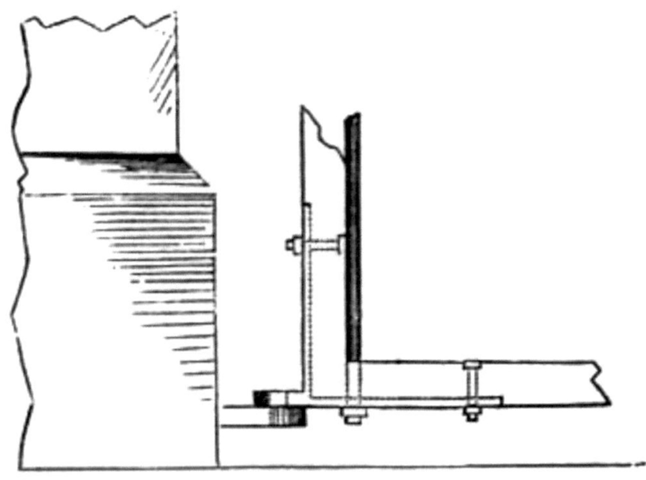

Fig. 88.

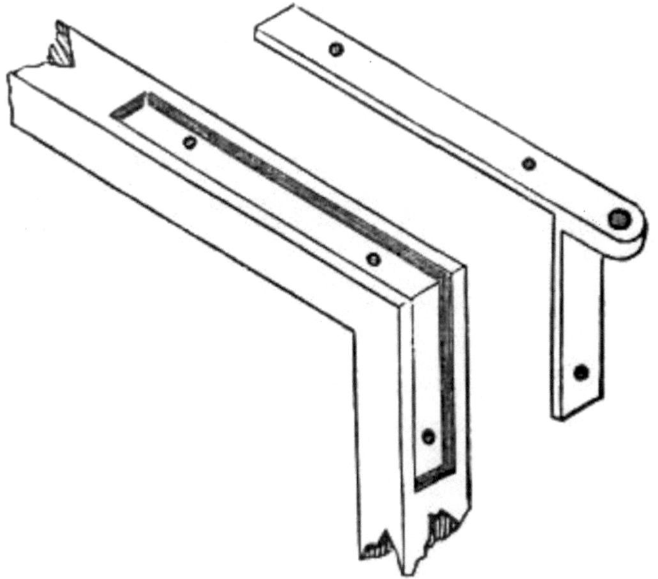

Fig. 89.

Figs. 87, 88, and 89, illustrate a novel style of hinge, peculiarly adapted to this gate, and is really stronger than any other. It requires less iron and less blacksmith work.

Fig. 87 shows the top hinge corner, and figure 88 the bottom hinge corner. The iron which secures this end of the gate, passes through both top and bottom hinge, and binds them and the gate securely together. The additional fastenings for hinge are made with carriage-bolts. Nothing but a power beyond the enormous tensile strength of iron and the compressible strength of wood, will cause the gates to yield in ordinary use.

Fig. 89 is a perspective view of the hinge, showing how it may be counter-sunk, and thus almost entirely concealed. Figs. 80, 81, 82, and 83, also show the hinge, and four different styles of stone gate piers.

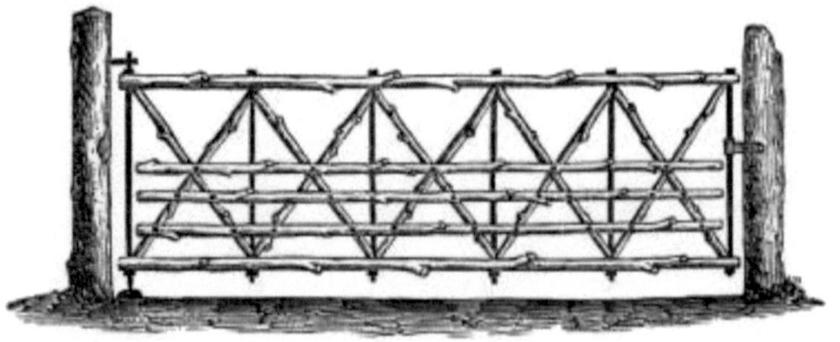

Fig. 90.

Fig. 90 is intended for a farm gate. The cross rails [129] [128] are secured by carriage-bolts passed through them and the main braces. Each end of the gate has an iron rod only, which is made heavier than the others, and saves framing. The hinge is made by having the iron rod project beyond the bolt head and nut, and the upper end is passed into an eye, as shown in Fig. 91, which is screwed into the post; the lower end is pointed, and is placed in a stone as shown, or it may rest on solid iron of similar form to the eye. Any intelligent laborer, with an axe and auger, can, with the iron work, make these farm gates.

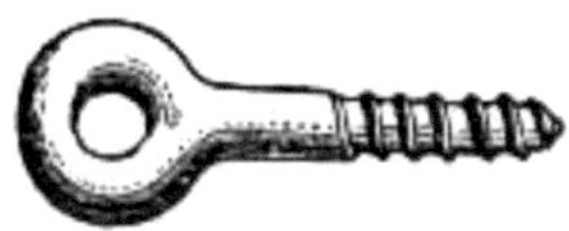

Fig. 91.

This principle of constructing gates admits of an infinite variety of designs; those given are merely suggestive. It admits of all classes of workmanship, from the plainest to the most elaborate, from the simplest farm gate to those required for the finished park, and in beauty, strength, and economy stands unequaled.

Fig. 92 and 93.—Plan and elevation of an entrance gate, which we have executed in oak, and presents an effective appearance. [130]

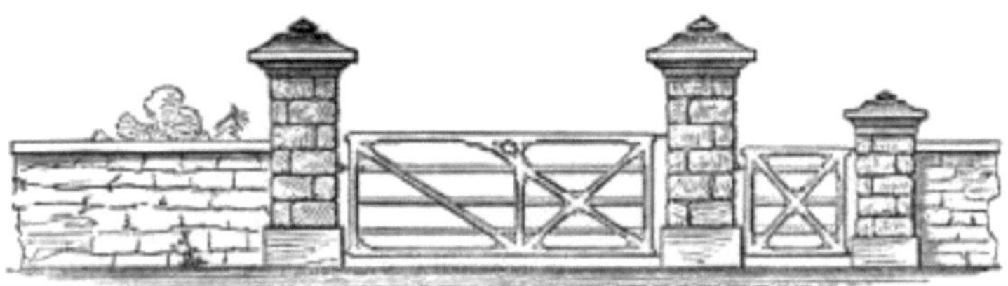

Fig. 92.—*Elevation of Entrance Gate.*

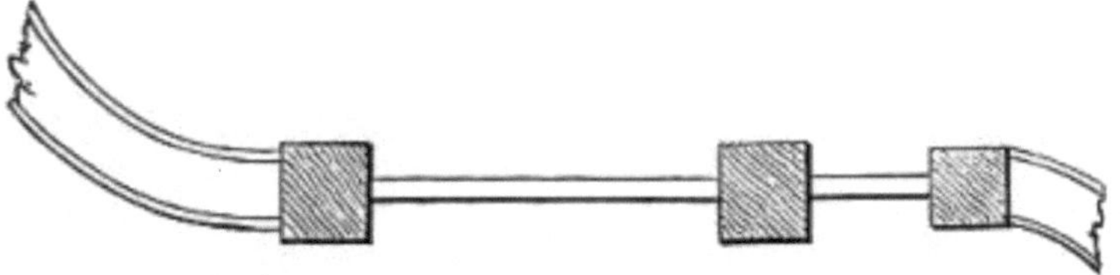

Fig. 93.—*Plan.*

[131]

DESIGN No. 28.

RESIDENCE OF TRISTRAM ALLEN, ESQ.,

RAVENSWOOD, N. Y.

The accompanying view of Mr. Allen's house is a good example of the method of adding to a dwelling which has ceased to be of sufficient capacity for the requirements of the family. By reference to the basement or cellar plan, the outline of the old house and the foundation of the new will be distinctly seen. The addition transforms the cottage to a villa, and in a manner which preserves the proportions as harmoniously as if the whole had been erected at one time and from one plan, thus illustrating a prominent advantage in this style of architecture, which admits more freely than any other, successive additions, which, when properly designed, add to the variety of outline, and its beauty of light and shade. The different floor plans show the arrangements of rooms and their connection with the original building, which, it will be seen, are convenient and compact.

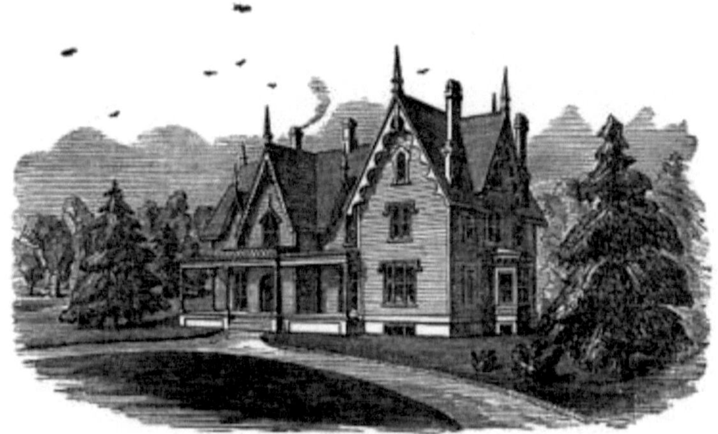

Fig. 94. — *Perspective.*

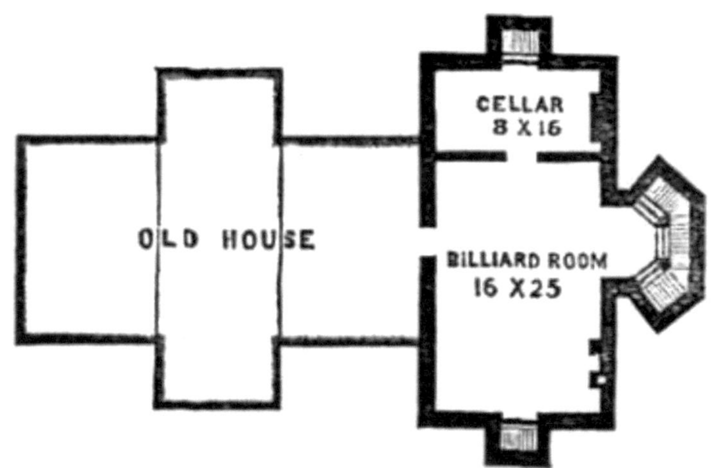

Fig. 95.—*Basement.*

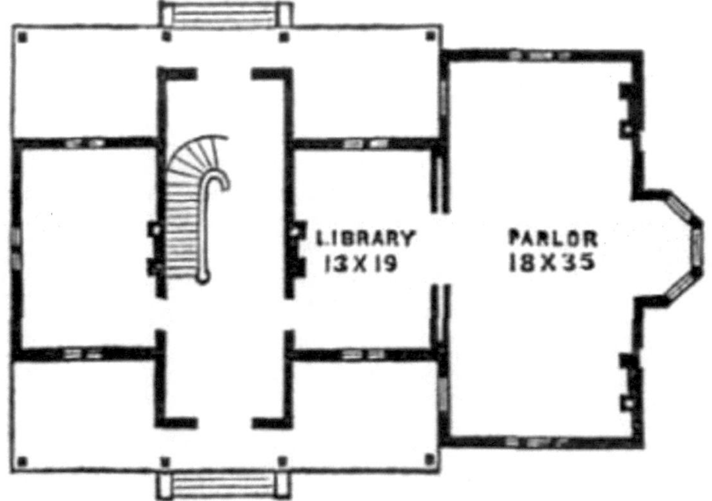

Fig. 96.—*First Floor.*

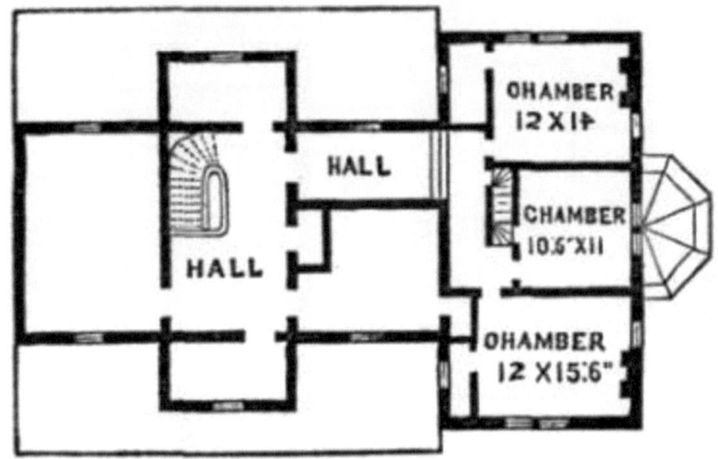

Fig. 97.—*Second Floor.*

Ravenswood is one of the most elegant of the suburbs of New York, being near at hand, and having frequent and rapid communication with the city. Situated on the Long Island shore, opposite the centre [134] [133] [132] of Manhattan Island, overlooking the great metropolis and its outlying cities, of easy access to the Central Park by the Hell Gate Ferry, amid all the refinement of fine gardens, polished landscape scenery, and architectural taste, it presents at once all the enjoyments that a combination of city and country life can afford.

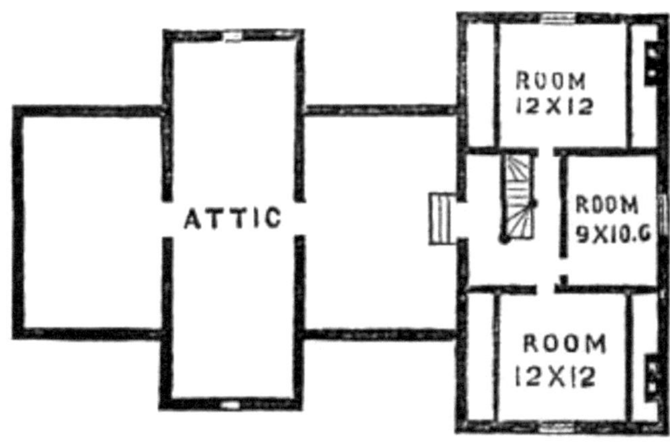

Fig. 98. — *Attic.*

DESIGN No. 29.

RESIDENCE OF LINDLEY M. FERRIS, ESQ.,

NEAR POUGHKEEPSIE, N. Y.

The residence of Mr. Ferris, of which we give the plans only, is located south of the city of Poughkeepsie, and almost or quite within its suburbs. The surrounding estate, of 150 acres of handsomely rolling land, possesses all the attractions of beauty and fertility so generally awarded to the finer portions of [135] Dutchess county. In the immediate vicinity are some of the highly finished and well-kept country seats which adorn this portion of the Hudson, and make up the attractions which taste and refinement always add to country life.

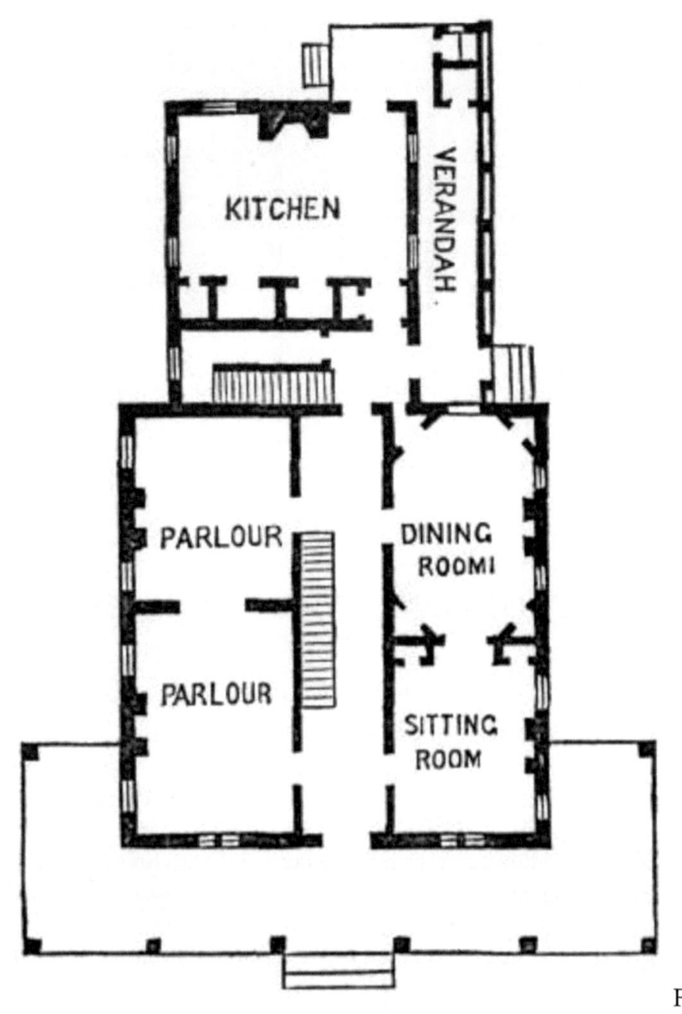

Fig. 99.—*First Floor.*

The object aimed at in the design of this house, was that of a substantial and commodious mansion, suited to the requirements of a large family, and that should express its purpose in the simplest manner at [136] a moderate expense. It was therefore desirable to

110

avoid all costly irregularity of form, and all the fanciful varieties of gimcracks.

The style selected as best illustrating this purpose is the Chateau roof, Louis XV style; the main building being 43 feet square, with a rear addition 25 by 29 feet; the plan illustrating the arrangement of rooms, verandah, etc. The first floor gives double parlors, (one of which may be used as a bed-room or library,) a sitting-room or reception-room, dining-room, and a large kitchen, with necessary closets, an inclosed verandah, water closets, etc. The second floor, main building, gives four large bed rooms and two smaller rooms for other purposes, and in the rear are four servants' rooms and a bath-room. The attic story, main building, has now five rooms, finished with closets, and two rooms more can be added by putting up two partitions. These upper rooms, in a roof of this character, are cool, well ventilated, well lighted, and agreeable in warm weather, there being roomy air chambers between the attic ceiling and the upper roof, and also between the walls of the rooms and the outer wall of the house. There is but little difference in the value of these rooms and those on the floor below, except convenience of access.

The house is built of brick, in a first class manner, the lower roof slate, the upper one being tin; is [137] thoroughly finished throughout, and is in all respects a convenient, durable, and commanding structure, giving the largest amount of room in a desirable and attractive form, with the most economy of means. It is situated on a knoll overlooking all the surrounding grounds, which include a number of other fine sites, one or two of which, we think, even more desirable than the one selected. It is not, however, an easy matter to choose one from a dozen sites, each almost equally good.

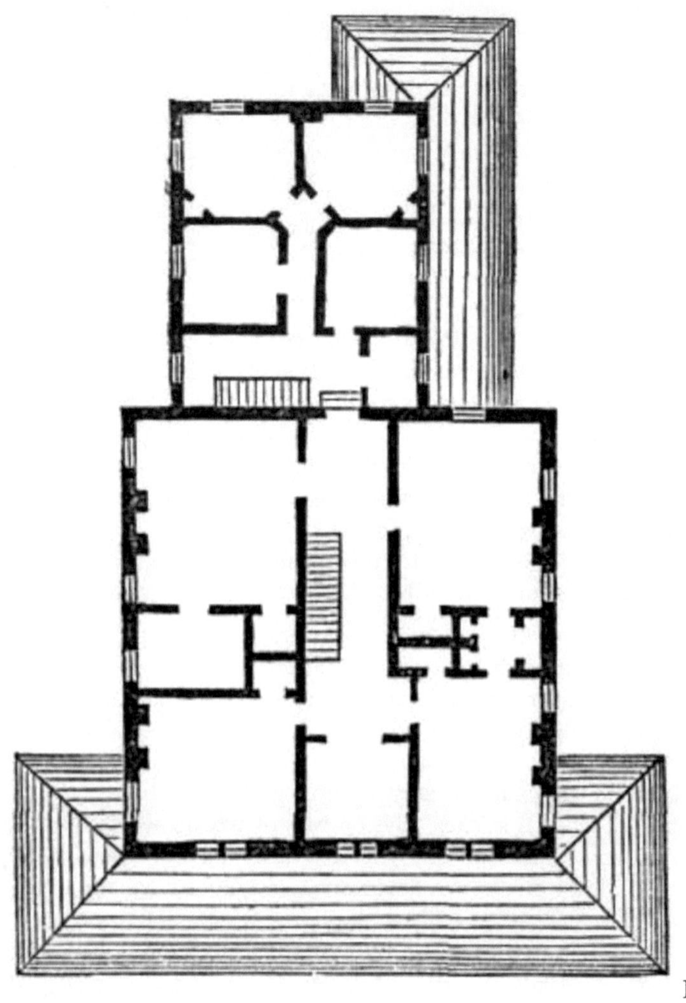

Fig. 100. — *Second Floor.*

[138]

A new road is now being laid through these and the adjoining premises, to connect two of the principal drives southward from Poughkeepsie, which when completed, will add a new attraction to the beautiful suburbs of this city. The views from the grounds, more particularly from the top of the house, are varied and extensive. The mountain panorama, which sweeps three-fourths of the horizon, beginning with the Fishkill mountains, and ending with the Catskills, is exceedingly fine. The eastern view embraces the Vassar Female College, the noble gift of Matthew Vassar, Esq., to the cause of female education. In the foreground and middle distance are the rich rolling landscapes of Dutchess and the fertile hillsides of Ulster counties, the glittering spires of Poughkeepsie, the lordly Hudson, and southerly are seen the famous Beacons and the Highland Pass,

> "Where Hudson's wave o'er silvery sands
> Winds through the hills afar."

[139]

DESIGN No. 30.

MODEL SUBURBAN COTTAGE – IN THE OLD ENGLISH OR RURAL GOTHIC STYLE.

BY FREDERICK S. COPLEY, ARTIST, TOMPKINSVILLE, S. I.

The general appearance of this Cottage, as seen from the road, is shown in the engraving, (Fig. 101.) which is a perspective view of the North and East Fronts.

It is situated at Montrose, on the lake-like shores of Hempstead Harbor, near the village of Roslyn, Long Island, a spot noted for its beauty and healthfulness.

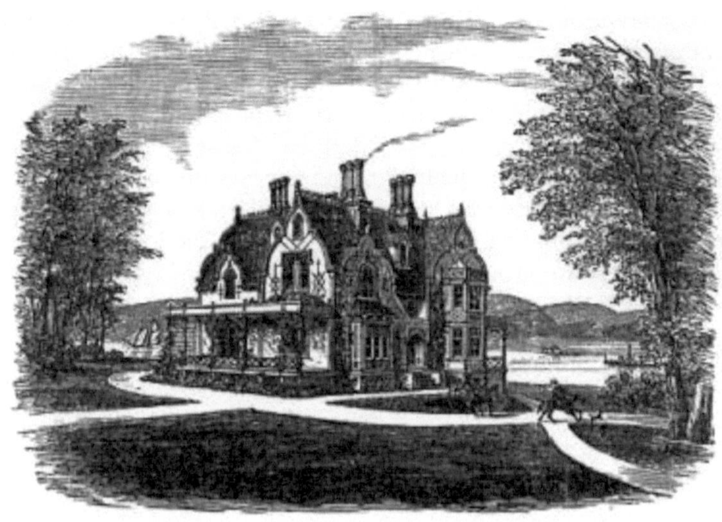

Fig. 101.—*Perspective.*

Size of building, 44 by 38 feet. Principal Plan (Fig. 103.) 10 feet high. P. shows a recessed porch, with double doors of oak, (oiled) the outer ones open, to be closed only at night and stormy weather, behind the one on the right is a space for wet umbrellas, &c., the inner doors have glazed panels to give light within, and should always be closed. V. is the vestibule, containing a spiral staircase, with walnut steps and rail (oiled). The floor laid with encaustic tiles, with ceiling groined, and walls finished in imitation of stone in the sand coat. On the left (under the stairs) is a private door opening into a lobby, fitted with [141] [140] wash-basin, water, &c., and lighted by a narrow window, that also serves to light the front basement stairs, so that a servant could answer a call, at either front or back doors, without passing through the central hall; which would not only be more convenient for them, but would be to the family and guests, especially in time of company, when the hall would form a central room, by closing the doors that lead to the stairs: nor would this interfere in the least with the domestics, or their duties: as they can go from cellar to attic without disturbing the privacy of a single room: and the guests could ascend, unseen to the dressing rooms above, (from either entrance) or depart in the same manner.

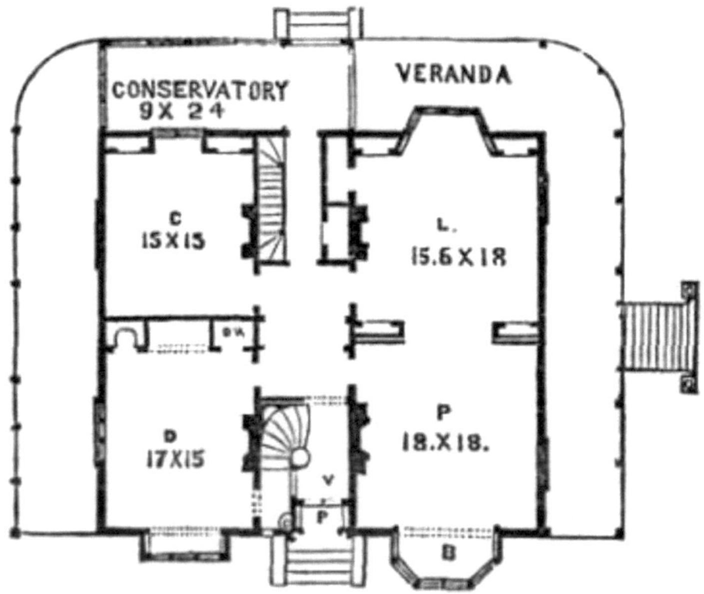

Fig. 102. — *First Floor.*

The hall screen, separating the vestibule, should be [142] of real oak, (oiled) and lighted in the panels with stained glass, which would impart a soft and pleasant light to the hall, and produce a fine effect on either side, day or night. The hall is here placed in the centre of the plan, and so happily arranged are the doors and rooms, as not only to give it a symmetrical effect, but to unite the whole, *en suite*, without disturbing the individuality of either. Also, the hall lamp and stove would light and warm, equally, every room, besides passage, vestibule, and stairs. The cloak closet is in the passage which contains the back stairs.

P. is the Parlor, which would be the favorite living room in the summer, as it faces the north, and has a large bay-window commanding a fine view down the harbor to the sound.

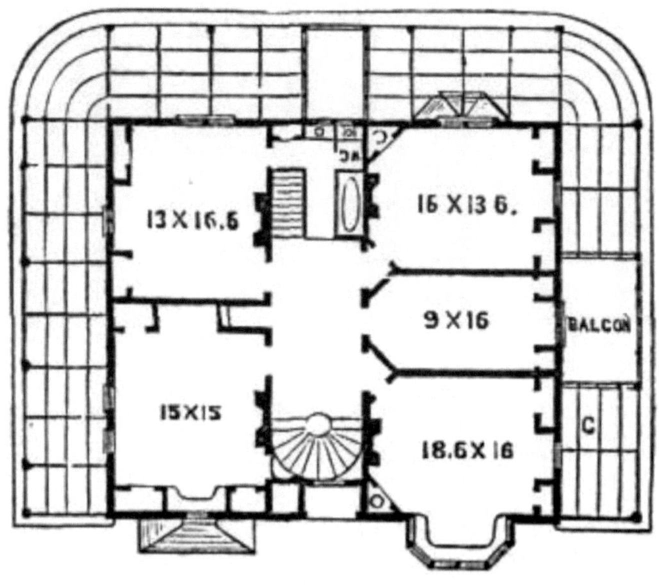

Fig. 103.—*Second Floor.*

L. is the Library, and living room, connected with the parlor by sliding doors, with recessed book-cases, on each side, and the same on the sides of the bay-window, here facing the south, and possessing a beautiful view of the bay and hills, with the village in the distance, which make it the favorite quarters in winter, being fully exposed to the genial influences of the sun during the absence of foliage at that season. On the right of the mantel is a private closet for plate, papers, &c., both these rooms have windows opening on the west veranda, with a fine view across the harbor. [143] D. is the Dining room, and a most cheerful one, (as it should be,) with a large ornamental window on the east, admitting the morning sun, and a fine bay-window on the north, looking down the road and harbor, possessing a charming prospect of land and water. To harmonize with the bay (on the other end) is the sideboard recess with a dumb-waiter on the right, and a china closet on the left; on one side of the mantel is the door opening into the lobby, which communicates with the hall, and basement plan below, and fitted with wash-basin, water, &c., which would be found most convenient to wash hands

116

or glasses, delicate or valuable articles of use not wished to be trusted to careless servants. It will be seen that the three bay-windows on this plan, are of different forms, and [144] each fitted with inside shutters. C. is the principal chamber, or boudoir, facing south and east, with fine large windows in each. The one on the south has closets on each side, and opens into the conservatory, making this a most delightful ladies'-work-room. It will be seen that all the rooms on this floor, although not large, are of the most comfortable size, perfect and elegantly proportioned, and arranged with every conceivable convenience requisite for the enjoyment of all the comforts and luxuries of life.

Chamber Plan (Fig. 103.) is nine feet high, and in keeping with the rest, in its admirable arrangements, furnishing five excellent rooms, with a bath room, convenient to all, fitted with the latest improvements, (the water closet enclosed, and vertical pipes, which would make freezing impossible). The four principal rooms are about equal in size and attractiveness, as they possess the same fine views as the corresponding ones beneath, and each finished with fire-places and ample closet room. The small room windows open on a balcony, with a charming view of the bay; and would afford an agreeable lounge in summer evenings, to enjoy the setting sun, or cool breeze. All the rooms on these two floors (except the last) to be fitted with Dixon's patent grates, and Arnott's ventilating valves, which would secure sweet, healthy, and warm rooms, without draughts. The hall, as will be seen, [145] is well lighted and ventilated, not only by the staircase window, on the north, but by the ventilating sash-lights over the doors of every-room; the bath room door is also lighted in the panel with ground glass. Between the doors, on the east side, is the lift, or dumb-waiter, and dust register, which being in the centre of the plan, is of equal convenience to all.

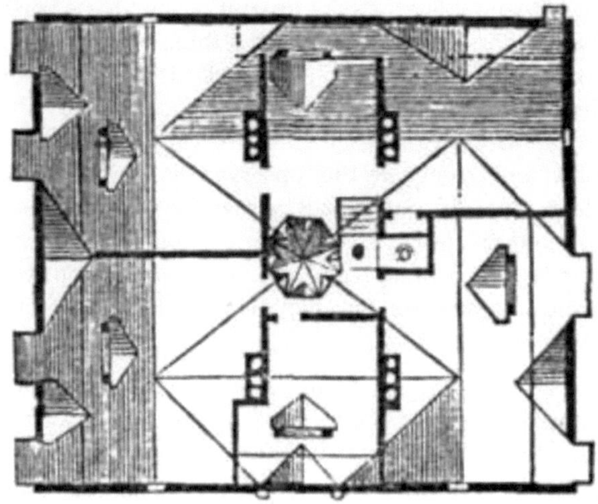

Attic and Roof.

Fig. 104. Roof and attic plan. The attic contains five good rooms for the accommodation of the servants, storing fruit, trunks, &c., and drying clothes. As this plan has the same central arrangements as all the rest, consequently the same advantages in economy of space, and of direct and easy access to every room, stairs, &c. The landing here is lighted in the same way as the hall below, and by the same staircase window, with the addition of a large sky-light and ventilator in the centre, which would keep the rooms sweet and cool. [146]

Fig. 105, shows the Basement and Cellar plan, nine feet high, and containing every requisite convenience for the domestic duties of a family. As they are on the same level, and under the principal story, the noise and smell of the kitchen would be excluded. The garden entrance is shown by the steps on the southwest corner of area, which extends the whole of the west side, round to the hall door on the south; and covered by verandah, would make these rooms dry, cool, and pleasant, as they are but little below ground, and well lighted on two sides, with a large bay-window in each; the north bay fitted with wash-tubs, as this kitchen is intended as a back one, or scullery, and for cooking in during the heat of summer, it has a sink closet on the left of the fire-place, and dresser and shelves for

118

pots and pans on the south side, by which, is a door opening into the basement, and one out on the area. The basement would be a cheerful room, facing the south with a large bay-window with seats and inside shutters, on the opposite side is a dresser fitted with plate rack, &c. On the east is the range and pantry; behind the range, in the hall, is a warm closet for clothes, shoes, &c., and opposite, under the stairs, is a dark one, for potatoes. At the north end of the hall, (and behind the scullery, fire-place, &c.) is the furnace room and front basement stairs. On the east side of the hall is the dumb-waiter, or lift. [147] The coal cellar has two bins placed under the shoots, for large and small coal, with two on the east side for ashes and wood. Against the middle window is a wire gauze safe, for cooked meats, &c.; between this and the wine cellar is the dairy; the other division is for stores in general. All the partitions are made open, so as to admit the free circulation of light and air.

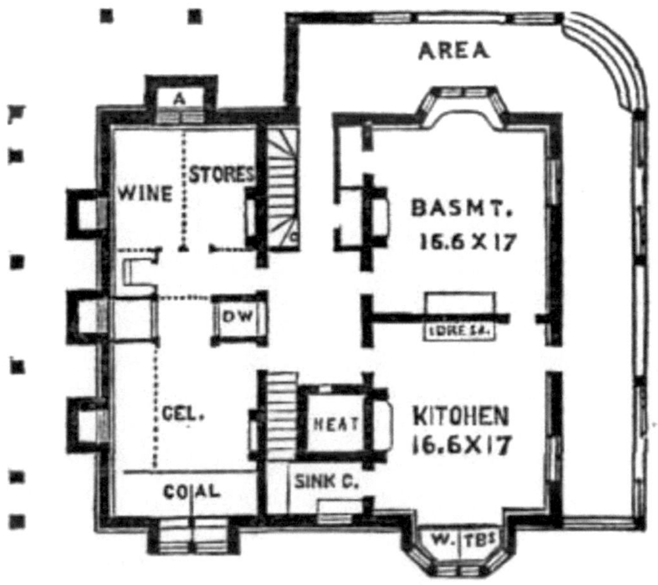

Fig. 105.—*Basement and Cellar.*

On observing the relative position of the different doors and windows, in the several plans, it will be found that the house may be ventilated by through drafts in every direction at pleasure; a luxury to be appreciated in the heat of summer. Also, by carrying the lift, or dumb-waiter, to the top of the house, and communicating with every floor, its full value would be secured, besides forming a ventilating shaft for the whole building, from cellar to attic. Another valuable [148] labor-saving convenience (next to the water-works and lift) is the dust shoot, which is simply a tin tube, with registers in the floors of the different plans, to sweep the dust into, from the rooms, where it descends to the cellar, and is caught in a barrel, to be removed when full. It is here placed in the hall, by the side of the lift, on every floor, which by this central arrangement is at the door of every room.

Construction, although of wood, is made nearly fire proof, by making the floors, walls, partitions and stairs solid. The walls and principal partitions are formed of slats of one inch thick by four inches broad, securely nailed one on the other, so as to form a one inch groove on both sides, to plaster on. This forms a good strong six inch solid wall, fire and vermin proof, and dryer than any built of stone or brick. The stairs to have their skeletons of iron work, filled in solid with cement. The floors of basement and entry to be of earthenware tiles, the kitchen and cellar cemented. That of the principal plan, (forming the ceiling of the basement, &c., the seat of danger,) should be formed of brick, arched on iron girders, and filled up with cement, and laid with larch, (as that burns less freely than any other wood). The hall, &c., to be laid with encaustic tiles. The floors of the chamber plans should have their timbers coated with plaster paris, and filled up with mortar and laid with [149] larch, the plastering of the ceilings, &c., on wire gauze, instead of lath; a slate roof, and the walls of the basement plan of hollow brick, and plastered on the inner surface. By these simple and inexpensive means, the house would be nearly fire proof, and life and property secure.

The exterior is covered by a sand coat, of a cheerful and rich light brown ochre tint, it being the most befitting for the situation and design, besides possessing the advantages of economy, and imparting a more substantial effect, it avoids that harsh and disagreeable glare and glisten of paint.

DESIGN No. 31.

The design on the following page, for a Head Stone, was published by us in the May number, 1864, of the Horticulturist. It attracted the attention of one of our most intelligent subscribers and valuable contributors in Western New York, who desired to set up, in their beautiful Cemetery, a memorial of one of his household who "who had gone before." The monument was executed in this city, under the supervision [150] of the friend who furnished the design for the Horticulturist. It was cut from the Caen stone, and the execution was every way satisfactory. The gentleman for whom it was made says in a letter advising of its safe arrival: — "Last week I had it set in a solid foundation, and my highest anticipations are more than realized. I do not see how the monument could be better, as to material, design, and inscriptions. It is unique, yet chaste, highly significant and satisfactory. I have only words of praise and feelings of gratitude for a result that so fully answers to my ideal."

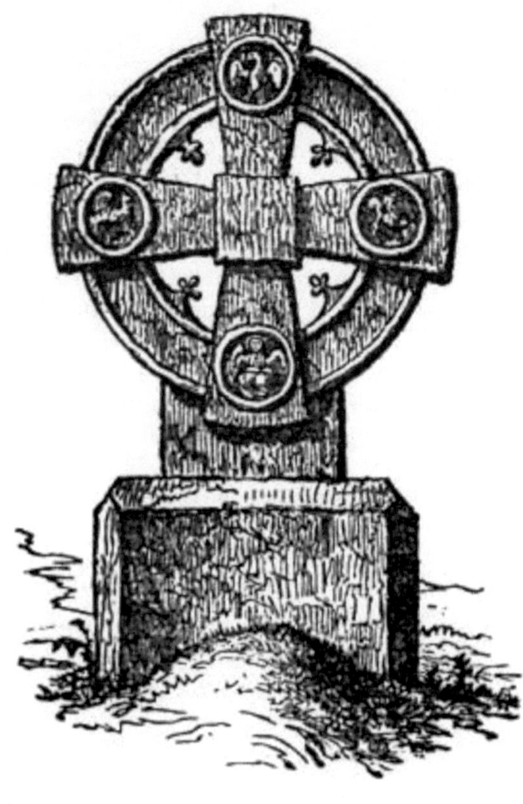

Fig. 106.—*Head Stone*.

[151]

"BALLOON FRAMES."

"If it had not been for the knowledge of balloon frames, Chicago and San Francisco would never have arisen as they did, from little villages, to great cities in a single year."—Solon Robinson.

In these days of Ballooning, it is gratifying to know that there is one practically useful, well tested principle, which has risen above the character of an experiment, and is destined to hold an elevated position in the opinions of the masses. That principle is the one which is technically, as well as sarcastically, termed Balloon Fram-

122

ing, as applied to the construction of all classes of wooden buildings.

The early history of the Balloon Frame, is somewhat obscure, there being no well authenticated statements of its origin. It may, however, be traced back to the early settlement of our prairie countries, where it was impossible to obtain heavy timber and skillful mechanics, and the fact is patent to any one who has passed through the pleasures and the vicissitudes of the life of a pioneer, that his own necessities have indicated the adoption of some principle in construction, that, with the materials he has at hand, shall fulfill all the necessary conditions of comfort, strength and protection. To these circumstances we must award the early conception of this frame, which, with [152] subsequent additions and improvements, has led to its universal adoption for buildings of every class throughout the States and cities of the West, and on the Pacific coast.

The Balloon Frame has for more than twenty years been before the building public. Its success, adaptability, and practicability, have been fully demonstrated. Its simple, effective and economical manner of construction, has very materially aided the rapid settlement of the West, and placed the art of building, to a great extent, within the control of the pioneer. That necessity, which must do without the aid of the mechanic or the knowledge of his skill, has developed a principle in construction that has sufficient merit to warrant its use by all who wish to erect in a cheap and substantial manner any class of wooden buildings.

Like all successful improvements, which thrive on their own merits, the Balloon Frame has passed through and survived the theory, ridicule and abuse of all who have seen fit to attack it, and may be reckoned among the prominent inventions of the present generation, an invention neither fostered nor developed by any hope of great rewards, but which plainly and boldly acknowledges its origin in necessity.

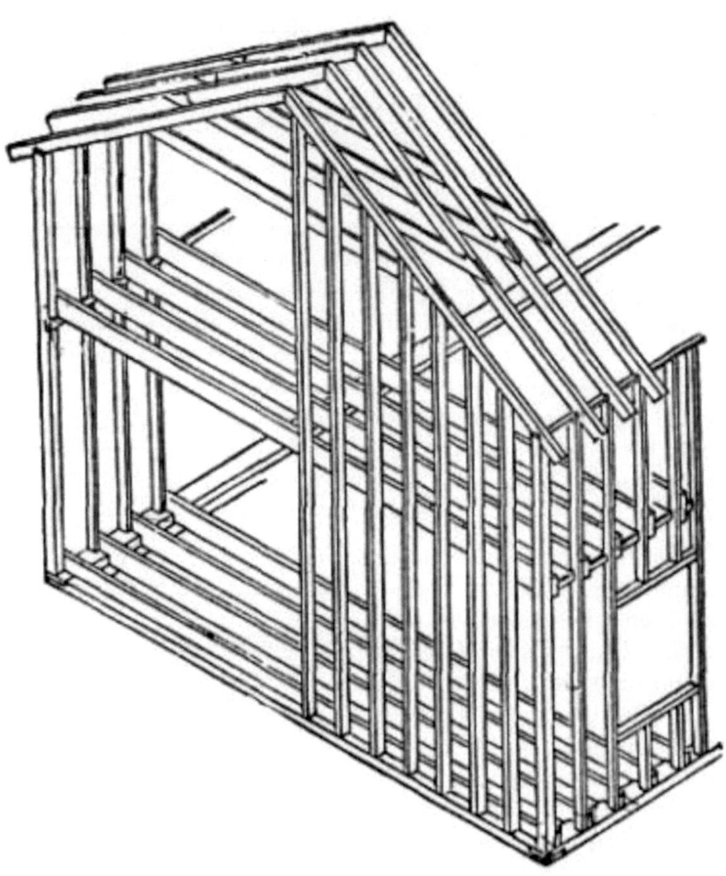

Fig. 107.—*Isometrical Perspective View of the Balloon Frame.*

The increasing value of lumber and labor, must turn the attention of men of moderate means to those successful plans which have demonstrated economy in [153] both, and at the same time preserved the full qualities of strength and security so generally accorded to the old fogy principles of framing, and which, we presume to say, is inferior in all the true requisites of cheap and substantial building. Light sticks, uninjured by cutting mortices or tenons, a close basket-like manner of construction, short bearings, a continuous support for each piece of timber from foundation to rafter, and embracing and taking advantage of the practical fact, that the tensile and compressible strength of pine lumber is equal to one-fifth of that of wrought [154] iron, constitute improvements introduced with this frame.

If, in erecting a building, we can so use our materials that every strain will come in the direction of the fibre of some portion of the wood work, we can make inch boards answer a better purpose than foot square beams, and this application of materials is one reason of the strength of Balloon Frames.

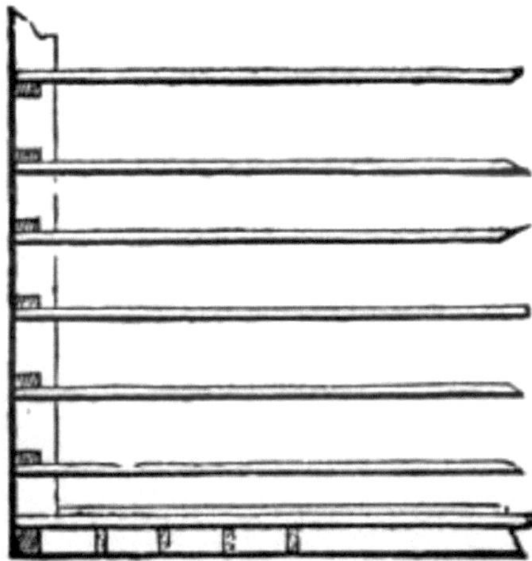

Fig. 108. — *Floor Plan.*

The Balloon Frame belongs to no one person; nobody claims it as an invention, and yet in the art of construction it is one of the most sensible improvements that has ever been made.

That which has hitherto called out a whole neighborhood, and required a vast expenditure of labor, time, and noise, can, by the adoption of the balloon frame, be done with all the quietness and security of an ordinary day's work. A man and boy can now [155] attain the same results, with ease, that twenty men could on an old fashioned frame.

The name of "Basket Frame" would convey a better impression, but the name "Balloon" has long ago outlived the derision which suggested it.

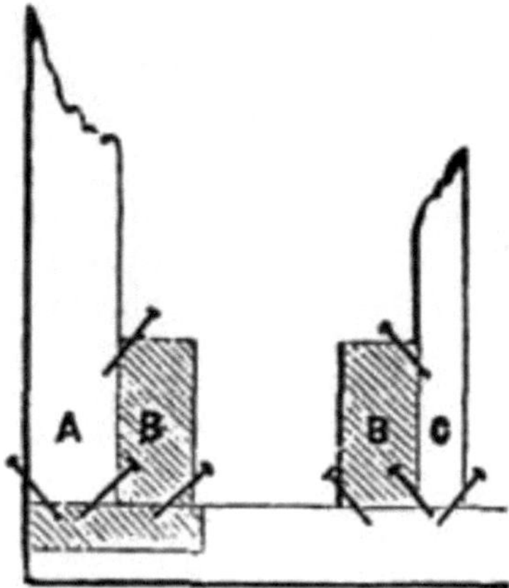

Fig. 109. — *Elevation Section —
manner of nailing — A. corner stud, 4 by 4 – B. joist, 3 by 8 – C. stud, 2 by
4.*

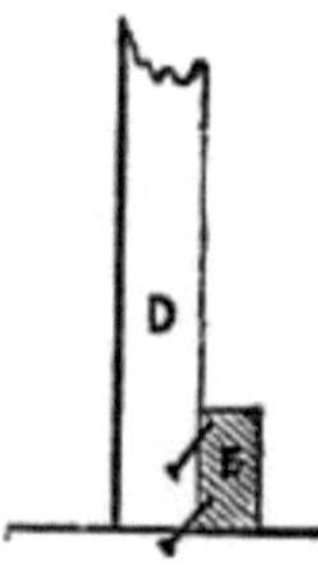

Fig. 110. — *D. Upper Edge of Joist – E. Stud.*

The moment the foundation is prepared, and the bill of lumber on
the ground, the balloon frame is ready to raise, and a man and boy
can do all of it. The sills are generally 3 inches by 8 inches, halved at
the ends or corners, and nailed together with large nails. Having
laid the sills upon the foundation, the next thing in order is to put
up the studding. Use 4 by 4 studs for corners and door posts, or
spike two 2 by 4 studs together, stand them up, set them plumb,
and with stay laths secure them in position. Set up the intermediate
studs, which are 2 by 4 inches, and 16 inches between centres, toe or
nail them diagonally [156] to the sill. Then put in the floor joists for
first floor, each joist to be placed alongside each stud, and nailed to
it and to the sill. Next measure the height to ceiling, and with a
chalk line mark it around the entire range of studding; below the

126

ceiling line notch each stud one inch deep and four inches wide, and into this, flush with the inside face of the studding, nail an inch strip four inches wide. This notch may be cut before putting up the studs. If the frame be lined on the inside, it will not be necessary to notch the strip into the studs, but simply to nail it to the studding; the object of notching the studding is to present a flush surface for lathing, as well as to form a shoulder or bearing necessary to sustain the second floor; both of these are accomplished by lining inside the studding — (for small barns and outbuildings that do not require plastering, nail the strip 1 by 4 to the studding) — on this rests the joists of the second floor, the ends of which come flush to the outside [157] face of the studding, and both ends of each joist are securely nailed to each stud; the bearing of the joist on the inch strip below is close by the stud, and the inch strip rests on a shoulder or lower side of the notch cut to receive it. This bearing is so strong that the joists will break before it would yield. Having reached the top of the building, each stud is sawed off to an equal height; if any are too short they are spliced by placing one on top of the other, and nailing a strip of inch board on both sides. The [158] wall plate, 2 by 4 inches, is laid flat on top of the studding, and nailed to each stud; the rafters are then put on; they are notched, allowing the ends to project outside for cornice, &c. The bearing of each rafter comes directly over the top of each stud, and is nailed to it.

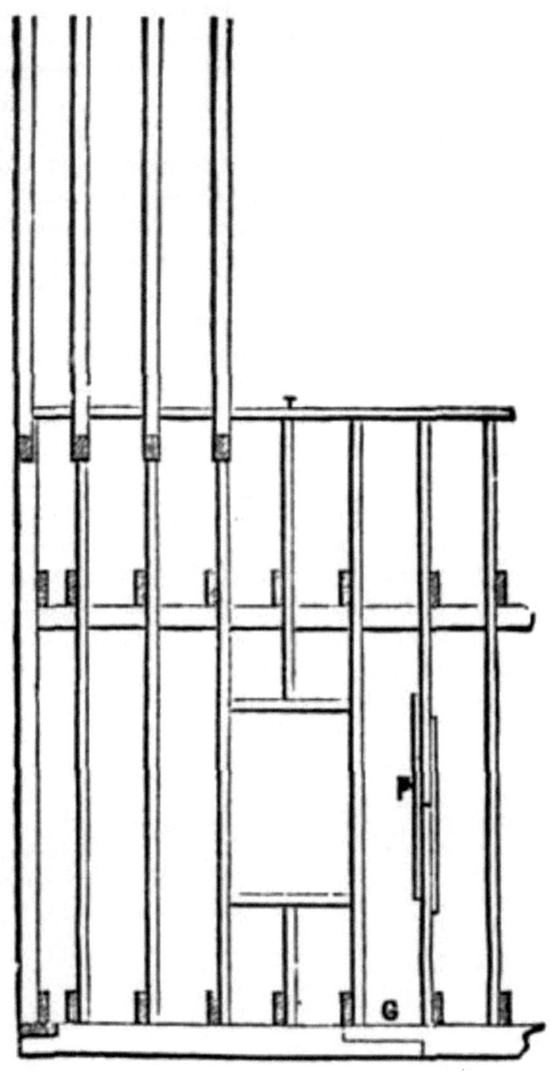

Fig. 111. — *Side Elevation. — G. Manner of splicing sills. — F. Manner of splicing studs.*

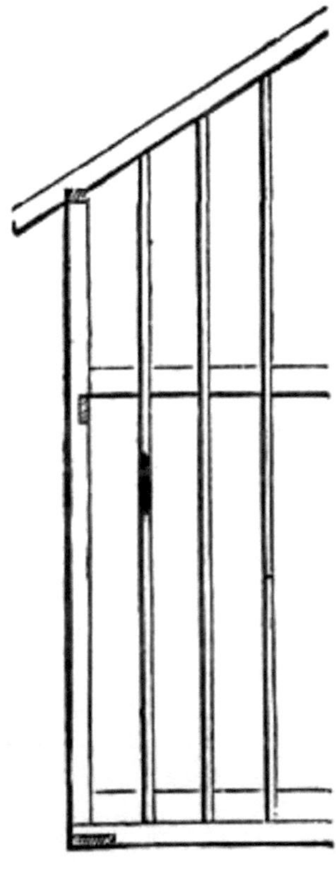

Fig. 112.—*End Elevation.*

A Balloon Frame looks light, and its name was given in contempt by those old fogy mechanics who had been brought up to rob a stick of timber of all its strength and durability, by cutting it full of mortices, tenons and augur holes, and then supposing it to be stronger than a far lighter stick differently applied, and with all its capabilities unimpaired. [159]

Properly constructed, and with timber adapted to its purposes, it will stand securely against the fury of the elements, and answer every purpose that an old fashioned timber frame is calculated to fulfill.

When the building is supported on posts, heavy sills are necessary, and the frame should be securely nailed or spiked together.

The bents may be 16, 24 or 30 inches apart, and covered in the usual manner. The thrust of both the rafters and contents of the building are outward; the tie, 1 by 4, is abundantly strong, as each one will practically sustain, in the direction of its fibre, three tons. The floor joists are nailed to studs at each end. No one need fear any lack of perfect security, as these ties exceed in strength any hold that tenons could have.

Fig. 113 illustrates the manner of framing buildings of one story, such as are used about almost every farm or country seat, as tool houses, granaries, wash-houses, spring houses, &c., &c.

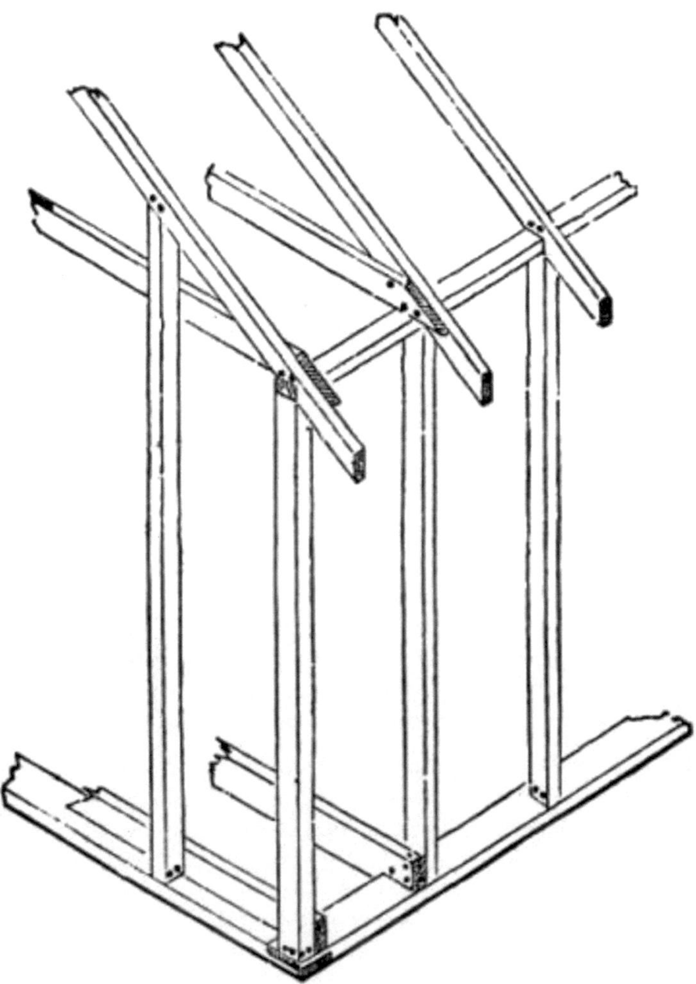

Fig. 113.—*Isometrical Perspective Balloon Frame.*

Very small buildings, if unplastered, will not require ceiling joists; a tie at each end will be all-sufficient. Moderate size buildings will be strong enough if the ceiling joists are left out, and collars put on half way up the rise of the rafter. According to the size and uses of the building, the collars or ceiling joists may be put on every rafter, every other, or every third rafter; floor joists should be about 16

[160] inches between centres, and the studding may be from 16 inches to 8 feet apart; in the last case only, every sixth floor joist is nailed to the stud, the intermediate ones being arranged equally distant from each other between the studding. Where the studding is placed wide apart, the plate must necessarily be heavier to sustain the roof; if vertical siding be used, it should be nailed to the sill and plate, and to an intermediate [161] horizontal strip spiked in between the studding; if done in this way, the plate may be lighter; when horizontal siding is used, the studding should not be more than 4 feet apart — in small buildings, say 12 by 20 feet, we should cut all our stuff, except joists, from 1¼ inch plank. Studs 4 inches wide, rafters 5 inches wide; floor joists should be 2 by 9 inches, and put all up 30 inches between centres.

In Fig. 114 is shown the manner of constructing frames for buildings of three stories. The corner stud, 4 by 4, is composed of and built up with two 2 by 4 studs, which are nailed together, breaking joints as the building progresses in height; the splicing of studs is done in the same manner, being nailed together as fast as additional length is required; the joists of the last floor are laid upon the plate, and they act as tie-beams to sustain the thrust of the rafters. We consider the splice where the studs butt and have side strips nailed to them, to be the most secure; the lapping splice is very generally used, however, and found to answer every purpose.

Ribs for vertical siding may be put on in two ways; one as shown, by which the ribs run over the sill, and are nailed to it; a strip of the same thickness as ribs, say 1¼ inches, nailed on to the sill to fill up the space between the ribs, and is then covered by the outside plinth or base. The other plan is to set the studs [162] back 1¼ inches from face edge of sill; then let the end of ribs bevel down on the sill, or dovetail them into the edge.

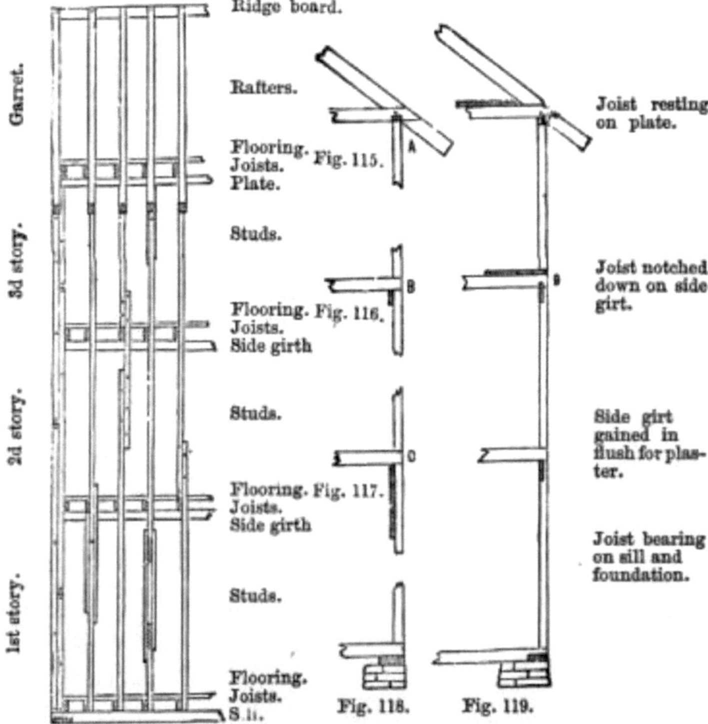

Fig. 114, Fig. 115, Fig. 116, Fig. 117, Fig. 118.

Either outside or inside lining may be used, or both together. Where diagonal lining is used, it should be reversed or run the other way on the opposite side of the house. [163]

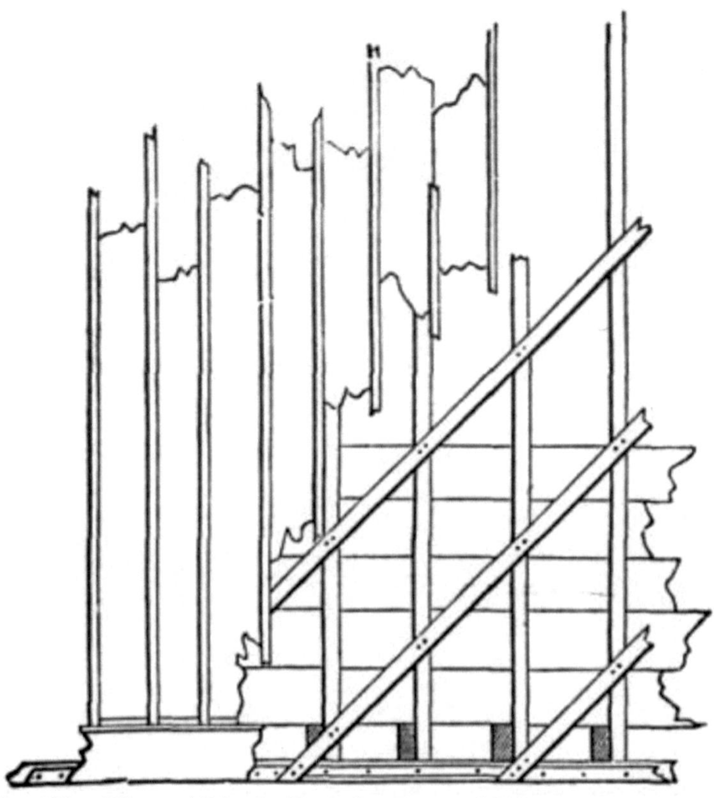

Fig. 120.—*Diagonal Ribs for Vertical or Battened Siding.*

The lining of a Balloon Frame adds immensely to its strength, particularly so if put on diagonally; it may be done outside or inside, though on the whole the inside is preferable. If done outside, it should be carried over the sill and nailed to it; the sill being wider than the studding, in order to get a larger bearing on the masonry, and the floor joists being in the way, does not admit of inside lining being put on in the same manner.

A first-class Balloon Frame should be lined, if for vertical siding, outside the studding—if horizontal [164] siding is used, line inside; it makes the frame stiffer and the building warmer. Some line diagonally, say from centre next the first floor towards extreme upper

134

corners both ways; others line one side diagonally in one direction, and the other in an opposite direction. This makes assurance of strength doubly sure. If lined inside, nail perpendicular lath to the lining 16 inches from centres, and on this lath horizontally for plastering.

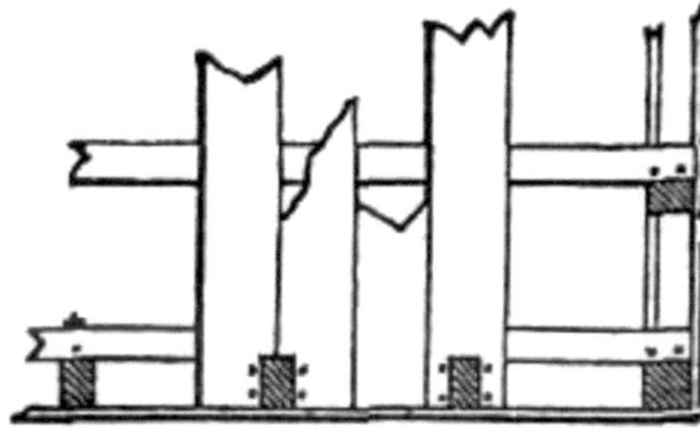

Fig. 121. — *Showing lengthwise and crosswise manner of tying frame.*

The principle of Balloon Framing is the true one for strength, as well as for economy. If a mechanic is employed, the Balloon Frame can be put up for *forty per cent. less money* than the mortice and tenon frame. If you erect a balloon frame yourself, which you can easily do without the aid of a mechanic, it costs the price of the materials and whatever value you put upon your own time.

Fig. 121 shows the manner of attaching the flooring to gable end studding, and in those buildings in which the thrust of the rafters is in the direction of the flooring—if every third stud be bolted to the joist [165] in the manner shown, it makes the tie equal if not superior to that in the direction of the joists.

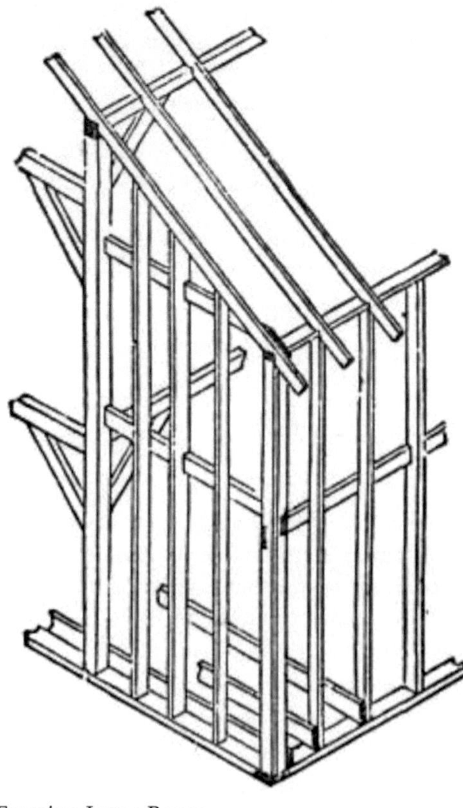

Fig. 122.—*Manner of Framing Large Barns.*

Fig. 122 explains the manner of framing the largest class of barns. Wide openings, like bays, require the use of heavy timber, and the mortice, tenon and brace, only so far as the gallows frame is concerned; the balance of the frame is of light stuff, studding 2 feet to 2½ feet apart, 2 by 6 inches, every third one 2 by 8 inches, into which is gained the side girt, it being nailed to the others. On this rests one end of the temporary floors, the gallows frame supports the roof, and the rafters are secured to it, so that they become ties. The side of this building is like a floor turned on edge, and is firmly secured by the floor joists at the bottom and the rafters at the top. [166]

136

Warehouses, depots, and other buildings of a very large size, can be made stronger by using the Balloon Frame, instead of the heavy timber frame. Those who prefer to err on the right side, can get unnecessary strength by using deeper studding, placing them closer together, putting in one or more rows of bridging and as many diagonal ribs as they like. In large buildings there is no saving in timber, only the substitution of small sizes for large—the great saving is in the labor, which is quite important.

The following are some of the advantages claimed for the Balloon Frame:

1. The principal labor of framing is dispensed with.

2. It is a far cheaper frame to raise.

3. It is stronger and more durable than any other frame.

4. Any stick can be removed, and another put in its place, without disturbing the strength of those remaining—in fact, the whole building can be renewed stick by stick.

5. It is adapted to every style of building, and better adapted for all irregular forms.

6. It is forty per cent. cheaper than any other known style of frame.

7. It embraces strength, security, comfort and economy, and can be put up without the aid of a mechanic.

[167]

Established in 1846.

- - - - -

"THE HORTICULTURIST,"

AND JOURNAL OF RURAL ART AND RURAL TASTE.

Published Monthly at Two Dollars and Fifty Cents per Annum, Twenty-five Cents per Number, and devoted to

GRAPE CULTURE,   FRUITS,
FLOWERS,   GARDENING,
RURAL ARCHITECTURE,   LANDSCAPE ADORNMENT,
AND RURAL PURSUITS.

Forming an annual volume of 400 royal octavo pages handsomely Illustrated.

The Author of *My Farm of Edgewood*,
The Author of *Ten Acres Enough*,
The Author of *The Grape Culturist*,
The Author of *Flowers for Parlor and Garden*,
The Author of *American Fruit Grower's Guide*.
Rev. Dr. Crescy,
and others of the best practical talent and ability, both East and West, write regularly.

Back Volumes and Numbers supplied.

GEO. E. & F. W. WOODWARD,
PUBLISHERS, 37 PARK ROW, N. Y.

WOODWARD'S GRAPERIES

AND

HORTICULTURAL BUILDINGS,

By Geo. E. & F. W. Woodward,
ARCHITECTS AND HORTICULTURISTS.

A new, practical, and original Work on the design and construction of all classes of Horticultural Buildings, including Hot-beds, Propagating Houses, Hot and Cold Graperies, Orchard Houses, Conservatories, &c., with the best modes of heating, &c. Elegantly Illustrated. Being the result of an extensive professional practice.

GEO. E. & F. W. WOODWARD,
PUBLISHERS,
Office of the "Horticulturist," 37 PARK ROW, N. Y.

[168]

GEO. E. & F. W. WOODWARD,

PUBLISHERS

No. 37 PARK ROW, NEW YORK

OFFICE OF THE HORTICULTURIST.

BOOKS

ON

AGRICULTURE,
HORTICULTURE,
ARCHITECTURE,
LANDSCAPE GARDENING,
AND RURAL ART

For Sale at this Office, or mailed, post paid, on receipt of Publisher's prices.

*** *Priced Catalogue on application.*

FIRE ON THE HEARTH.

— — — —

GEO. E. & F. W. WOODWARD,

37 PARK ROW, N. Y.

New York Agents for Dixon's low down Philadelphia Grates, for burning Wood or Coal, for sale at Manufacturer's Prices.

"It is a plan for warming houses, which has never in all its points been surpassed." *   *   *   *   *   *

"It is believed that there is scarcely a single educated Physician in Philadelphia, who owns the house he lives in, who is not supplied with one or more of these delightful luxuries." *   *

"We have one of these admirable contrivances, put in our house in 1859, and every additional year only increases our appreciation of the luxury." — *Dr. W. W. Hall, editor of Hall's Journal of Health, N. Y.*

Price $35 and upwards according to size and finish. Samples at this Office.